Edgar Brinsmead

The History of the Pianoforte

With an Account of the Theory of Sound and also of the Music...

Edgar Brinsmead

The History of the Pianoforte
With an Account of the Theory of Sound and also of the Music...

ISBN/EAN: 9783744768221

Printed in Europe, USA, Canada, Australia, Japan

Cover: Foto ©ninafisch / pixelio.de

More available books at **www.hansebooks.com**

THE HISTORY OF THE PIANOFORTE

WITH AN ACCOUNT OF THE

THEORY OF SOUND & ALSO OF THE MUSIC
AND MUSICAL INSTRUMENTS OF
THE ANCIENTS.

BY

EDGAR BRINSMEAD.

LONDON:
NOVELLO, EWER & CO.,
1, BERNERS STREET (W.), AND 80 & 81, QUEEN STREET (E.C.)

MDCCCLXXIX.

LONDON:
PRINTED BY NOVELLO, EWER AND CO.,
69 & 70, DEAN STREET, SOHO, W.

PREFACE.

IN writing the "History of the Pianoforte" I have endeavoured to give the fullest particulars regarding a subject interesting to every one who possesses the "Drawing-room Orchestra," by which name the piano has been aptly designated.

Although some millions of pianofortes have been manufactured in Great Britain, France, Germany, and America, it is surprising how few pianists know anything respecting the theory, construction, and history of their favourite instrument.

If I have succeeded in even partially supplying the information required, the labour of love that has engaged my careful attention during the last ten years will not have been undertaken in vain.

In preparing this new edition, I found it necessary not only to carefully revise the original work, but also to rewrite many portions of it which were manifestly imperfect. I have also added Part I. (on "Sound"), in compliance with the criticisms and suggestions which the former editions had evoked. I must gratefully acknowledge my indebtedness to Professor Tyndall, who has most kindly permitted me to copy many of the illustrations contained in his work "On Sound." In Part I. much valuable information has been gathered from the works of Chladni, Herschel, Helmholtz, and Tyndall.

The principal fields of thought from which material for the earlier chapters of Part II. has been gleaned are the Histories of Music by Dr. Burney and Sir John Hawkins, the works of Forkel and Carl Engel on ancient music and musical instruments, and the descriptions by Wilkinson, Rosellini, and Dr. Lorimer, of the latest discoveries in connection with these subjects. In the concluding chapters much has been derived from the writings of Fétis, Pole, Thalberg, Pauer and Dr. Rimbault.

Although I have spent much time in the study of works on music and musical instruments, it is not merely as a theorist that I write. I bring to my subject practical experience as a pianoforte manufacturer, and this gives me hope that, in explaining it to admirers of the pianoforte, I may be in some slight degree assisting the advancement of the art I so dearly love.

EDGAR BRINSMEAD.

June, 1879.

INDEX.

	PAGE
Preface	vii

PART I.—SOUND.

CHAPTER I.
Sound, Noise, and Music — — — — — 1

CHAPTER II.
On the Transverse Vibrations of Tuning-forks, Rods, Plates, and Bells — — — — — 16

CHAPTER III.
The Vibrations of Strings — — — — — 30

PART II.—HISTORY OF THE PIANOFORTE.

CHAPTER IV.
The History of Music — — — — — 56

CHAPTER V.
Stringed Musical Instruments of the Ancients — — 69

CHAPTER VI.

The First Instruments with the Pianoforte Keyboard—the Clavicytherium, Clavichord, Virginal, Spinet, Harpsichord, etc. - - - - - 84

CHAPTER VII.

The Invention and Progress of the Pianoforte - - 107

CHAPTER VIII.

Progress of the Pianoforte from its Introduction into England - - - - - - - - 117

CHAPTER IX.

Invention and Progress of the Upright Pianoforte - 133

CHAPTER X.

Useful Hints upon selecting, and practical directions for Tuning Pianos and Repairing small defects - 144

APPENDICES.

A—List of British Pianoforte Improvements Patented between the years 1693-1879 - - - - 153
B—Description of Dove's Sirene - - - - 189
C—Description of Notes on Sound - - - - 194

PART I.—SOUND.

CHAPTER I.

SOUND, NOISE, AND MUSIC.

SUCH perfect unity is displayed throughout the whole of the laws of Nature, that no branch of Physics can be studied without including much which at first sight appears to have no connection with it. Thus, an intimate acquaintance with the laws that govern radiant heat, light, and water in their motion, reflection, and refraction, will also give a clear insight into many of those connected with the transmission, reflection, and refraction of sound.

For instance, when a child watches the circlets of miniature waves produced by the stone he has thrown into a smooth piece of water, he takes a first step, by analogy, in the study of the theory of sound-waves. Many useful lessons may be taught to this little "father of the man" by means of his innocent pastime; as waves of sound and waves of water are nearly allied to each other in various ways.

When the surface of the water is in a state of great tumult, it bears a close resemblance to the disturbed state of the atmosphere that produces the discordance termed noise. When the peaceful wavelets radiate from the point at which the stone strikes the water, their motion is closely analogous to the regular and periodic pulsations of air that produce the sensation of a musical sound.

To thoroughly understand the difference between a noise and a musical sound, it is necessary to comprehend the distinction just set forth. Both are conveyed to the brain by means of the auditory nerve; but they produce entirely separate and distinct sensations.

The motion imparted to the air by any moving body produces a corresponding wave in the air that is in its immediate vicinity before it sinks to rest again, and this transmits a still feebler motion which is reproduced, with lessening force, in the contiguous air until the pulsations either die away or are met by some solid body that changes their course. Motion is thus conveyed from particle to particle, and when any of these are driven against the tympanic membrane (which is stretched across the passage leading from the orifice of the ear towards the brain) it sets it in motion. This motion is transmitted to the end of the auditory nerve, and along that nerve to the brain, where the sensation of sound is produced.

Professor Tyndall illustrated this in an extremely homely manner. In his excellent work, "On Sound," he writes :*—

"I have here five young assistants, A, B, C, D, and E (Fig. 1, p. 3), placed in a row, one behind the other,

FIG. 1.

TYNDALL'S ILLUSTRATION.

each boy's hand resting against the back of the boy in front of him. E is now foremost, and A finishes the row behind. I suddenly push A, A pushes B, and regains his upright position; B pushes C, C pushes D, D pushes E; each boy, after the transmission of the

---

* "On Sound." By John Tyndall, D.C.L., LL.D., F.R.S. 1875. P. 4.

push, becoming himself erect. E, having nobody in front, is thrown forward. Had he been standing on the edge of a precipice he would have fallen over; had he stood in contact with a window he would have broken the glass; had he been close to a drum-head he would have shaken the drum. We could thus transmit a push through a row of a hundred boys, each particular boy, however, only swaying to and fro. Thus, also, we send sound through the air and shake the drum of a distant ear, while each particular particle of the air concerned in the transmission of the pulse makes only a small oscillation. But we have not yet extracted from our row of boys all that they can teach us. When A is pushed he may yield languidly, and thus tardily deliver up the motion to his neighbour B. B may do the same to C, C to D, and D to E. In this way the motion might be transmitted with comparative slowness along the line. But A, when pushed, may, by a sharp muscular effort and sudden recoil, deliver up promptly his motion to B, and come himself to rest; B may do the same to C, C to D, and D to E; the motion being thus transmitted rapidly along the line. Now this sharp muscular effort and sudden recoil is analogous to the *elasticity* of the air in the case of sound. In a wave of sound, a lamina of air, when urged against its neighbour lamina, delivers up its motion and recoils, in virtue of the elastic force exerted between them; and the more rapid this delivery and recoil, or, in other words, the greater the elasticity of the air, the greater is the velocity of the sound."

When the vibrations of air are sufficiently rapid and perfectly periodic a musical sound is the result; but, when these vibrations are irregular in force and unperiodic, the sensation of noise is produced upon the brain through the auditory nerve.

In 1705 the philosopher Hawksbee proved before the Royal Society, that air is absolutely necessary to the propagation of sound. He placed a bell in the receiver of an air-pump, so that the air could be withdrawn whilst the bell was continually struck. When the air was almost exhausted scarcely any sound could be heard; but the experiment was not quite successful, as a perfect vacuum was not obtained.

When, however, the air has been completely withdrawn from a glass-vessel, no sound is audible, although the stroke on the bell can be plainly seen, and a clear ringing tone is heard directly the glass-vessel is refilled with air. *The intensity* of a sound, therefore, depends on the density of the air in which the sound is generated, and not on that of the air in which it is heard. Thus, a pianoforte heard in a rarefied atmosphere appears to lose much of the intensity of its tone; indeed, if the chamber were completely filled with a light gas, such as hydrogen, the sound would be almost inaudible. Sound, like radiant heat and light, is a wave-motion, and like them it may be conveyed to a distance without greatly impairing its intensity.

Biot, the celebrated French philosopher, found that he could hold a conversation in a low voice through an iron tube (one of the empty water-pipes of Paris) 3,120 feet in length, and that the slightest whisper was distinctly heard at that distance. This is accounted for by the fact that the air pulsations or waves, instead of flowing in all directions, are concentrated into a comparatively small column by the reflecting interior surface of the pipe.

Curved roofs and ceilings also act as reflectors of sound, as mirrors do of light and radiant heat. Sir John Herschel, in illustration of this fact, says that "the confessional of a cathedral in Sicily was so placed that the whispered confessions of the penitents were reflected to another part of the building. This was accidentally discovered by a man, who often amused himself and his friends by listening to these confessions of guilt. He, however, heard secrets from his wife's lips which completely marred the pleasures that he had previously derived from his eavesdropping."

The velocity of sound through gases and liquids may

be deduced from the compressibility of these, determined by proper measurements.*

Noise produces the effect of an irregular succession of shocks to the listener through the jarring upon the

---

* Dulong calculated that the velocities of sound through the following gases at the temperature of 0° centigrade are—

	Feet per Second.
Air...	1,092
Oxygen...	1,040
Hydrogen...	4,164
Carbonic Acid...	858

The velocities through liquids, according to Wertheim, are:—

	Temperature. Centigrade.	Feet per Second.
River-water (Seine)...	15°	4,714
Solution of Common Salt...	18°	5,132
,, Chloride of Calcium	23°	6,493
Common Alcohol...	20°	4,218

The same authority gives the velocity of sound through solids at the following rates:—

	At 20°C. Feet per Second.	At 100°C. Feet per Second.	At 200°C. Feet per Second.
Lead...	4,030	3,951	—
Gold...	5,717	5,640	5,619
Iron...	16,822	17,386	15,483

WOOD.

	Along Fibre.	Across Rings.	Along Rings.
Acacia...	15,467	4,840	4,436
Fir...	15,218	4,382	2,572
Beech...	10,965	6,028	4,643
Oak...	12,622	5,036	4,229
Pine...	10,900	4,611	2,605
Elm...	13,516	4,665	3,324
Sycamore...	14,639	4,916	3,728
Ash...	15,314	4,567	4,142
Elder...	15,306	4,491	3,423
Aspen...	16,677	5,297	2,987
Maple...	13,472	5,047	3,401
Poplar...	14,052	4,600	3,444

auditory nerve; but a musical sound flows regularly and with perfect smoothness, rendering the impulses received by the tympanic membrane perfectly periodic. The production of a musical sound, in fact, depends upon the action of a body that moves with the regularity of a pendulum.

If the air-waves produced by this motion follow each other with sufficient rapidity and regularity, the tympanic membrane and the auditory nerve are kept continually in motion, for a body once shaken does not sink to rest immediately.

Continuous impulses will thus produce the impression of a musical sound. Galileo generated a musical sound by drawing a knife over the edge of a piastre, as a sonorous continuity of taps was thus produced. If the puffs of a locomotive engine were repeated at the rate of fifty or sixty in a second, an organlike tone would be the result. It follows that musical sounds can be produced by rapidly and regularly sustained taps or puffs of any kind. The production of musical sounds by the taps of the rotating teeth of a cogged wheel against a card was first illustrated by Robert Hooke. This was afterwards perfected by the Frenchman, Savart, a drawing of whose invention is given in Fig. 2, p. 9.

This machine consists of a wheel covered with

FIG. 2.

FIG. 3.

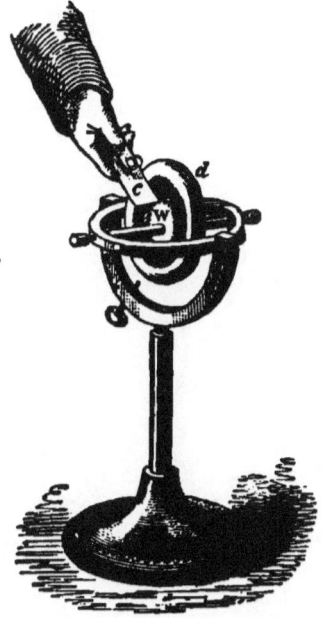
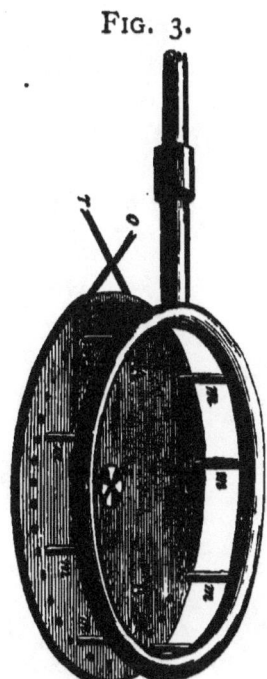

SAVART'S GYROSCOPE.

SEEBECK'S SIRENE.

numerous teeth, and is made to rotate very rapidly by means of a band. When a playing-card is held against the teeth as the wheel revolves slowly, a succession of taps is heard; but when the wheel is made to rotate rapidly these blows are no longer discernible, as a musical sound alone is perceptible. When the revolutions are exceedingly rapid a treble note is the result, and as these revolutions are gradually slackened this pitch slowly flattens.

From this invention, it is apparent that *the pitch of a note is dependent upon the rapidity of its vibrations.* Professor Robison proved the fact by means of a series of puffs of air. He writes: "A stopcock was so constructed that it opened and shut the passage of a pipe 720 times in a second. The apparatus was fitted to the pipe of a conduit leading from the bellows to the wind-chest of an organ. The air was simply allowed to pass gently along this pipe by the opening of the cock." The repetition of this 720 times in a second produced the note G in alt, and at 360 times per second a harsh tone like that of a man's voice was the result. This discovery led to the invention of the sirene, a description of which instrument will doubtless be interesting, as its apparatus determines the number of air-puffs per second necessary to the production of any note.

The sirene was made in a very simple manner by August Seebeck, as represented in Fig. 3, p. 9. It consists of a pasteboard disc, about twelve inches in diameter, in the margin of which are holes of equal size, placed at regular intervals around the circumference. The disc is made to revolve very rapidly on its axis by means of a whirling table to which it is attached.

Immediately over the circle of holes is placed the bent tube, m. When the disc revolves slowly, the perforations are brought successively under the tube, allowing the free passage of the air which is blown through it. When the disc is made to rotate rapidly, the puffs follow each other in such quick succession that the air-pulsations produce a musical sound.

When the rotations are very rapid a shrill treble note is produced. When they are gradually slackened, the puffs of air through the tube give musical sounds of lower and lower pitch; until, at last, only the puffs of air themselves are heard as they pass through the perforations.

The pasteboard sirene has been greatly improved by Dove, whose instrument is a rather complicated one. This apparatus has a register, by means of which the rapidity of vibration of any sonorous body may be accurately measured, whether it be an organ-pipe, a

Fig. 4.   Fig. 5.

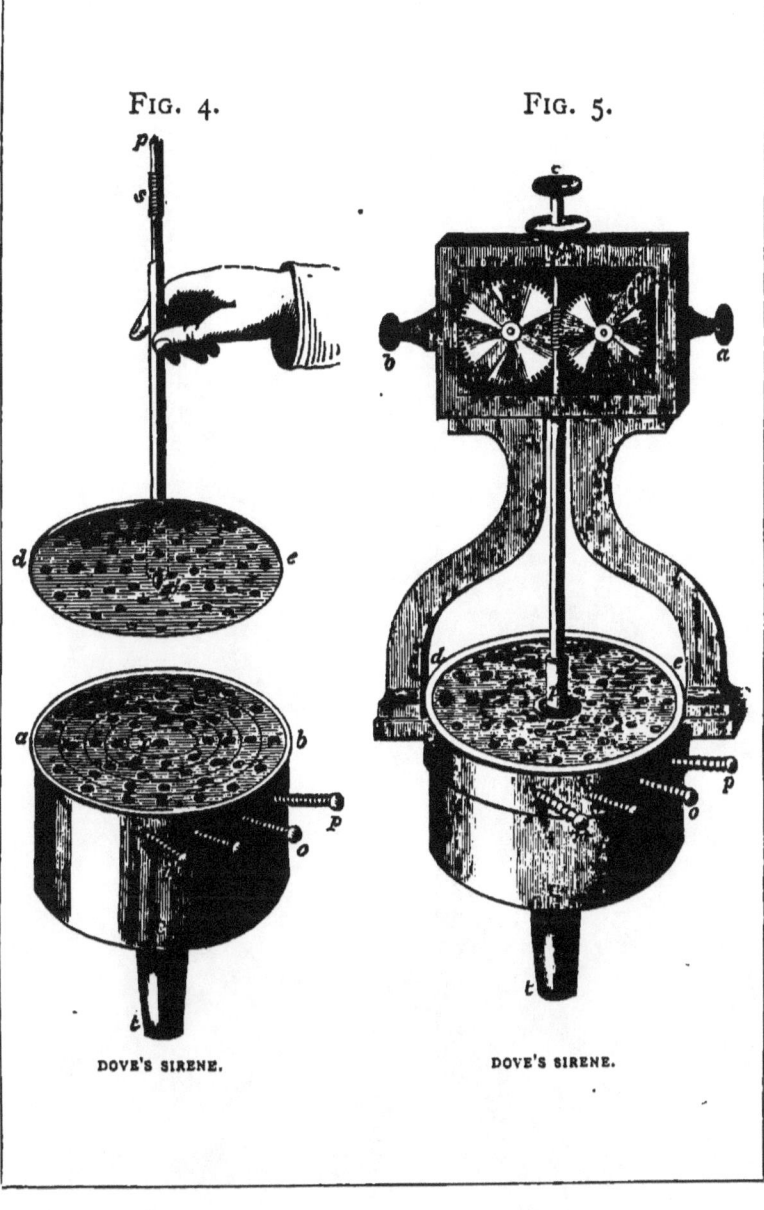

DOVE'S SIRENE.   DOVE'S SIRENE.

reed, the human voice, a vibrating string, or a tuning-fork. It is divided into four series of orifices instead of the one set that Professor Seebeck employed.

Dove's sirene is shown in Figs. 4 and 5, p. 13, which are fully described in Appendix C, p. 293. By doubling all the parts of Professor Dove's instrument, Helmholtz, in his "double sirene," has greatly increased its power.

CHAPTER II.

ON THE TRANSVERSE VIBRATIONS OF TUNING-FORKS, RODS, PLATES, AND BELLS.

A TIGHTLY drawn string or wire, when set in rapid motion, will communicate pulsations to the air at perfectly regular intervals; and a tuning-fork, whether set in motion by means of a bow or by a blow, will produce a precisely similar effect. The prongs, when in intense vibration, produce a clear musical sound which gradually diminishes in intensity as the amplitude of these vibrations becomes lessened; the rate of vibration being always the same, and the pitch consequently remaining without alteration.

If a copper wire be attached to the prong of a tuning-fork, it will vibrate in unison with the fork. If the vibrating prong then be gently let down to a glass table previously smoked or covered with soot, it will then sing its own history, which will be faithfully registered in marks upon the glass as the fork is slowly drawn across it; but when the fork is kept in the same position, the prong simply vibrates along the same line. When the vibrating fork is drawn gently along the glass a curved line is plainly marked by its progress, and this sinuous line gradually forms itself into a straight one as the amplitude of the vibrations gradually diminishes.

By means of a looking-glass, Lissajous was enabled to reflect the beam of intense light that he threw upon the marks formed by the tuning-fork; and this reflection was shown upon a screen placed at a suitable distance, the luminous wave on the screen rendering visible the exact vibrations of the fork.

A wave of sound is produced by the prongs of the tuning-fork advancing and retiring; as the condensation and rarefaction thus produced in the air are the necessary constituents of a sonorous wave— the wave of sound being measured from one condensation to the succeeding condensation. Any two bodies vibrating with the same rapidity will produce tones similar in pitch, for pitch is solely determined by rapidity of motion, whether in a string, a tuning-fork, a reed, or in the human vocal chords; therefore the number of vibrations propelled by any of these can be exactly determined by the pitch of the sound produced. The sound-wave ordinarily generated by the speech of a man is from eight to twelve feet, and that of a woman is from two to four feet, in length; thus producing an interval of about an octave between the two voices.

This interval of an octave is proved by the sirene to be due to the fact that the number of vibrations proceeding from the woman's voice is exactly double the number of those proceeding from the man's voice. Thus an octave must have exactly double the number of vibrations of the fundamental note. Commencing, for example, at a note of 150 vibrations, it may be proved that the octave to this fundamental note will be 300, the second 600, the third 1,200, the fourth 2,400 vibrations per second.

Savart, by his toothed wheel (Fig. 2, p. 9), proved that the ordinary limit of human hearing is 24,000 vibrations per second; but Helmholtz fixes the limit at 38,000 in the upper and sixteen vibrations per second in the lower register of hearing. The sense of human hearing is thus proved to be wisely limited to about eleven octaves; for, were the almost infinite vibrations of insects' wings audible, the sound of the growth of grass, trees, and flowers, as well as the circulation of the blood and sap in all of these, would produce a roar simply appalling.

Dr. Robert Hooke, in writing upon this subject, observes, " Who knows, I say, but that it may be possible to discover the motions of the internal parts of bodies, whether animal, vegetable, or mineral, by the sound they make; that one may discover the works performed in the several offices and shops of a man's body, and thereby discover what instrument or engine is out of order, what works are going on at several times and lie still at others, and the like; that in plants and vegetables one might discover by the noise the pumps for raising the juice, the valves for stopping it, and the rushing of it out of one passage into another, and the like."

The sense of hearing varies greatly in different listeners; but whenever the number of vibrations is increased beyond the limit of his hearing, insensibility to that sound at once ensues. For instance, the extreme treble notes of an organ, the chirrup of a cricket, and the squeak of a bat, are quite inaudible to many people. Sir John Herschel writes, "Nothing can be more surprising than to see two persons, neither of them deaf, the one complaining of the penetrating shrillness of a sound, while the other maintains there is no sound at all." Thus the chirruping of sparrows and the hum of insects are inaudible to many persons whose sense of hearing is perfectly acute to noises of lower pitch.

Sir Charles Wheatstone proved, in a very interesting manner, that sound will pass through solid bodies. He placed a piano at the bottom of his house, and allowed a tin tube, in which long deal sticks had been placed, to rest upon the sounding-board of the instrument. These sticks were carefully joined together and passed to the top of his house. When the piano was performed upon no sound was audible in the upper room, until the sounding-board of a harp, violin, or some other musical instrument was connected with the upper end of the deal rod. Directly this connection had been made, the sound of the piano became audible in the upper room, the tone produced being very harplike in quality. The pulsations were necessarily conveyed to the sounding-board through the deal rod.

The vibrations produced by a tuning-fork placed on a small wooden box can be conveyed to another wooden box by corresponding means.

A rod, when fixed at both ends, vibrates throughout its entire length, at half, and at a quarter of its length, and it can divide its vibrations into even still smaller parts. When it divides into halves, each of these vibrates with nearly three times the rapidity of the whole. These vibrations of a rod fixed at both ends are maintained by its own elasticity without any external tension. When a rod is fixed at one end and left free at the other, it will divide into vibrating segments. If it be struck sharply the entire oscillation is feeble, and the partial oscillations between the nodal points are executed with vigour; but when the stroke is sluggish the whole oscillation is well marked, and the nodal divisions are not plainly discernible. Of these nodes or points of division, in vibrating rods and strings, more will be said in the next chapter.

If the vibrating rod produced a musical sound, the division into two vibrating parts by its central node would produce the first overtone to its fundamental tone. The shorter these rods are made the more acute will be the tone produced by them when set in vibration, as the number of vibrations executed in a given time is inversely proportional to the square of the length of the vibrating rod. If, therefore, a rod be doubled in length the vibrations will then be reduced to one-fourth; by trebling it the rate of vibration is reduced to one-ninth; and by quadrupling the length the rate of the vibrations is reduced to one-sixteenth.

Chladni took a rod, three feet in length, which vibrated once in a second. He then reduced it to one foot, and the result was nine vibrations per second. When he reduced it to six inches, the rod vibrated thirty-six times; at three inches 144 times, and at one inch it vibrated 1,296 times a second.

Chladni's discovery led to the invention of the "iron fiddle," made in Paris. This instrument was simply a wooden tray, in which were fixed small iron rods of varying lengths arranged in a semicircle. When a violin-bow set these pins in vibration musical sounds were produced, but the effect was not sufficiently pleasing to induce performers to practice this description of violin-playing.

Small strips of metal fixed at one end are also used in the musical box. The overtones or nodal divisions of a vibrating rod rise very rapidly, for, from the first division onwards, the rates of vibration are approximately proportional to the squares of the series of odd numbers, 3, 5, 7, 9, 11, &c. Thus, if the vibrations of the whole rod be thirty-six, then the vibrations corresponding to this and to its successive divisions would be approximately expressed by the series of numbers— 36, 225, 625, 1,225, 2,025, &c.

Sir Charles Wheatstone, by the use of his simple instrument, the kaleidophone, produced on a screen the beautiful scrolls that are represented in Fig. 6, p. 23. These were formed by the vibrations of a rod fixed at one end, to which light silvered glass beads were attached. The characters resulting from the vibrations were thrown on the screen by means of a strong light.

Chladni proves that if a rod be free at both ends its deepest tones are higher than the deepest tones of a rod of equal length fixed at one end in the same proportion as four to twenty-five. In Mozart's opera "Die Zauberflöte" a little instrument, composed either of wooden or glass rods, free at both ends, is used to imitate a peal of bells, and the effect is

Fig. 6.

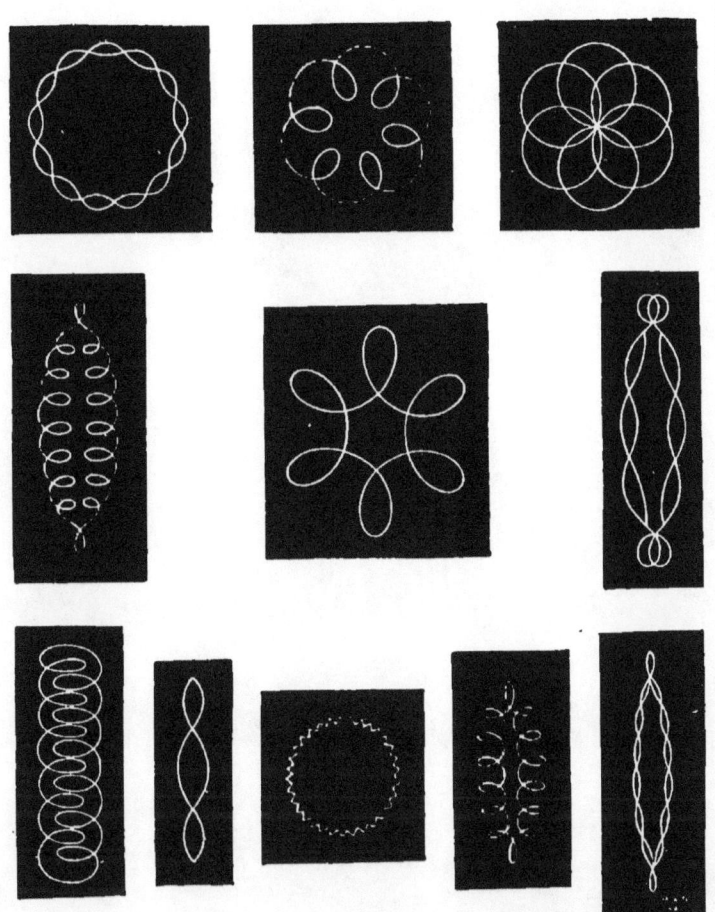

SIR CHARLES WHEATSTONE'S LUMINOUS FIGURES PRODUCED BY THE
KALEIDOPHONE.

very musical. When wooden rods are used this instrument is called the "straw fiddle," because the rods usually rest at their nodes on twisted straw. Chladni, in 1785, tried a great number of experiments with rods and plates. He says, "The experiments on the electric figures formed on a plate of resin, discovered and published by Lichtenberg,* in the Memoirs of the Royal Society of Göttingen, made me presume that the different vibratory motions of a sonorous plate might also present different appearances if a little sand or some other similar substance were spread on the surface. On employing this means, the first figure that presented itself to my eyes upon the circular plate already mentioned resembled a star with ten or twelve rays; and the very acute sound in the series alluded to was that which agreed with the square of the number of diametrical lines." He held a plate of glass at its centre by means of a clamp, and, after sand had been scattered over its surface, a corner of the plate was first damped by touching it with the finger-nail, and then set in vibration by means of a violin-bow. This vibration threw aside the sand, which then collected along the two nodal lines.

---

* Lichtenberg had made the experiment of scattering an electrified powder over an electrified resin-cake, the arrangement of the powder thus revealing the electric condition of the surface.

When the plate was damped in the middle of one side and the plate was set in vibration at that point, the sand formed itself into a diagonal figure. This note, Chladni found, was a fifth above the previous one. When two other points were damped and the bow had been drawn across the centre of the opposite side of the plate, a still higher note was produced, and the sand marked the nodal lines.

Many beautiful examples of the scrolls obtained in this manner, by damping different parts of the plate, are shown in the frontispiece.

Sir Charles Wheatstone analysed the vibrations of square plates in a very complete manner. He found that square pieces of glass or of sheet-metal obey the same laws as free bars and rods.

The results obtained by the vibrations of circular plates are also very beautiful. The rate of vibration of these discs is directly proportional to their thickness, and inversely proportional to the square of their diameter. Thus, if two circular plates are of equal thickness, and the diameter of the second disc be double that of the first, the pitch produced from each will be that of an octave to the other. If the thickness of the two plates be precisely the same, but the diameter of one be half that of the other, the same result of the octave will be obtained when both are in vibration. Chladni discovered that when he rendered the centre of the disc free and damped appropriate points of the surface, nodal circles and other curved lines were produced in the sand with which he lightly covered the vibrating plates.

When a point has been damped, and a violin-bow at the distance of forty-five degrees from this point causes the plate to vibrate, the fundamental note is produced. If white sand has been previously scattered over the blackened surface of the glass plate, the nodal lines will be plainly seen dividing the surface into four quarters. When the bow is drawn across the disc at thirty degrees' distance from the point damped, the sand at once arranges itself in the form of a star, thus showing that six vibrating segments are separated from each other by these nodal lines. By drawing the bow at points that are still nearer to the place damped by the finger and thumb holding the plate, the disc can be made to divide itself into eight, ten, twelve, fourteen, or sixteen sectors, with their appropriate nodal lines between them. As these divisions become more minute, the vibrations are proportionately accelerated, and the pitch of the note produced is raised until an extremely shrill sound results. By rendering the centre of the disc free, and damping appropriate points of the surface, nodal circles and other curved lines may be obtained.

The nodes and vibrating segments of a bell are similar to those of a disc, the division into four vibrating sections towards the crown of the bell forming the fundamental note. The same rules that have been given respecting the division of vibrating discs and respecting the thickness of these plates are also applicable to bells. Like a disc also, a bell can divide itself into any even number of segments, but not into an odd number. Thus, if the vibrations of the fundamental note be forty, that of the next higher tone will be ninety, of the next 160, the next 250, the next 360, and so on.

Chladni, by experimenting on an ordinary tea-cup, proved that it divides itself, like a bell, into four vibrating segments when a fiddle-bow is drawn across its edge. He also found that the handle had a material influence on the tone produced. When the bow is drawn over the point exactly opposite to the handle, and when the point is ninety degrees from the handle, the same note is heard; as the handle in both these cases is in the centre of a vibrating segment, loading it with its weight. When the bow is drawn over a point forty-five degrees distant from the handle the note is sensibly higher than before, as the handle then occupies a node instead of loading the vibrating segment, as in the previous instance.

When bells are made of thin metal the tendency to subdivision is so great that it is almost impossible to bring out the pure fundamental tone without the admixture of the higher ones. Bells often have varying thicknesses round their sound-bows, and these produce the same effect as the handle of the cup in the experiment just described. This will account for the intermittent sound when the higher tones are gradually dying out; as this effect is produced through the varying thickness of the metal in the bell, which causes the different segments to vibrate unequally.

CHAPTER III.

THE VIBRATIONS OF STRINGS.

STRETCHED metal wire, when fixed at both ends and tightly drawn over a sounding-board, as in the pianoforte, is capable of intense vibration. The vibration of strings may be studied either on elastic cords loosely stretched, which are not sonorous, but enable the experimentalist to see their motion; or else on the sonorous strings of the pianoforte, guitar, or on the monochord.

In the first instance the strings can be made of thin spirals of brass wire of about six to ten feet in length. When gently stretched and fastened at both ends this string will move with great regularity if set in vibration by the finger. The string may be first vibrated as in Fig. 8, p. 31. In this instance a single fundamental tone is produced, without harmonics or overtones. The string may, however, assume the forms of Fig. 12, B, C, and D, p. 37. In this case the form of the string is that of two, three, or four half-waves of a

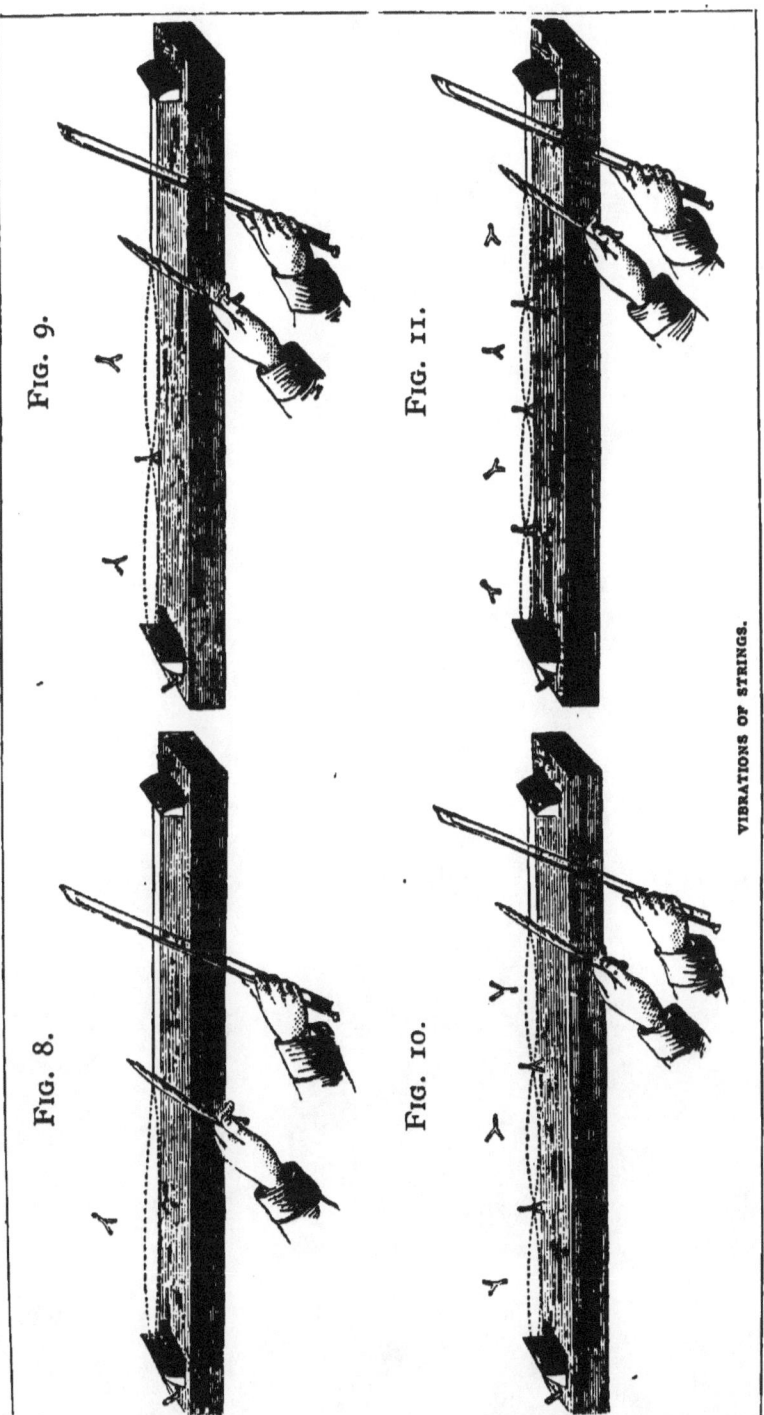

VIBRATIONS OF STRINGS.

simple wave curve. In the form B the string produces only the upper octave of its prime tone; in the form C the twelfth, and in the form D the second octave. The dotted lines show the position of the string at the end of half its periodic time.

In B the point b remains at rest; in C two points, c_1 and c_2, remain at rest; in D three points are at rest, leaving the sections e, d_1, d_2, d_3 in vibration. These points are called *nodes*. The nodes, or points of rest, may be plainly seen in a vibrating spiral wire, and in an ordinary pianoforte they may be found by placing small pieces of twisted paper along the strings. When the string is set in vibration the whole of these paper riders will be thrown off, as in Fig. 10, p. 31, with the exception of those placed upon a nodal point, at which place the string is at rest. The centre of the string is the first nodal point; and if it be pressed lightly with a goose quill, the string will be at once divided into two equal lengths, each of which will produce the octave tone to the fundamental notes sounded by the entire length—its number of vibrations being twice as rapid as the prime tone. If the string be divided into three equal parts, by lightly touching these nodal points the vibrational number of each of these sections will be tripled; if into four, the vibrations will be quadrupled in rapidity, and so on.

The nodal points can be easily discovered by placing some paper riders on the string, as in Fig. 9, p. 31; for a strong vibration will overthrow all the riders that are not astride these points of rest. In this illustration the two riders that are not on the nodal point are tossed off, whilst the third sits quietly astride the point of rest. In Fig. 10, p. 31, two riders keep their seats between the three ventral segments, whilst the others are overthrown. If the string be damped with the finger at one-fifth of its length the vibrating string will unhorse the four riders placed on the ventral segments of the vibrating string (Fig. 11, p. 31), whilst the three that have been placed on the nodal points retain their seats.

To set a spiral wire in these various forms of vibration it should be moved periodically at one of its extremities with the finger. Its lowest number of vibrations give the prime tone A (Fig. 12, p. 37); twice this number will show the node B; three times the rate will show the nodal point C; and four times will give the nodal point D. When the finger is placed lightly on any of these points of rest, and the string is pulled between that point and the nearest end, the other nodes then appear directly the vibrations commence.

For instance, if the node 1 in C or 1 in D be kept at rest by the finger, the string will show the other nodes after it has been twanged at E. In this illustration the vibrational forms of a resonant string are illustrated. To obtain these in a pure form tuning-forks should be struck, and the handle held on the sounding-board near the string, which will then vibrate in sympathy with it. By pressing the finger lightly upon any one of the nodes all the simple vibrations are damped, excepting those that have a node at this point; as those alone remain which allow the string to be at rest in this place.

Very fine strings give a greater number of nodes than the thicker ones, which are more rigid. In the bass strings of a grand pianoforte, tones with ten sections may be easily produced; and if the strings are extremely light, as many as twenty segments may be obtained. These vibrations, which are like the oscillations of a pendulum, excite in the ear only the perception of a simple tone. They are not, however, simply pendular, when the string is excited by the friction of a violin-bow; by plucking, as in harp-playing, or by the stroke of a pianoforte hammer, as the vibrations are then compounded of many simple vibrations, which taken separately correspond to those in Fig. 12, p. 37.

The multiplicity of these composite forms of motion is infinitely great; the string may, indeed, be considered as capable of assuming any form (provided very small deviations from the position of rest be closely adhered to). Any given form of wave can be compounded out of a number of simple waves. The bass strings of a pianoforte therefore allow of a great number of these compound upper partial tones (which are usually termed *harmonics*), especially when the instrument is lightly strung. These are discernible as high as the sixteenth, after which harmonic they are so closely intermixed as not to be plainly separable. Thus, when a bass string has been struck, the upper strings which correspond to the divisions of the second, third, fourth, &c., upper partial tones will vibrate in sympathy with them, unless checked by the dampers.

In experimenting with the pianoforte a horizontal grand or a square instrument should be selected. When the top has been raised, a small chip of wood should be placed on one of the bass strings. If this has been placed on one of the ventral segments it will immediately be jerked violently into the air. For instance, when one of the lower tones of C is struck, as C, F, C, A flat, F, D, or C, the motion is much less violent when one of the harmonic tones of C is struck, as C, G, or C, in which case the piece of wood will not move if placed exactly over one of the nodal points. These nodal points may be easily discovered by pressing the string lightly with the finger and thumb upon both sides of the string. When the key is struck a dull,

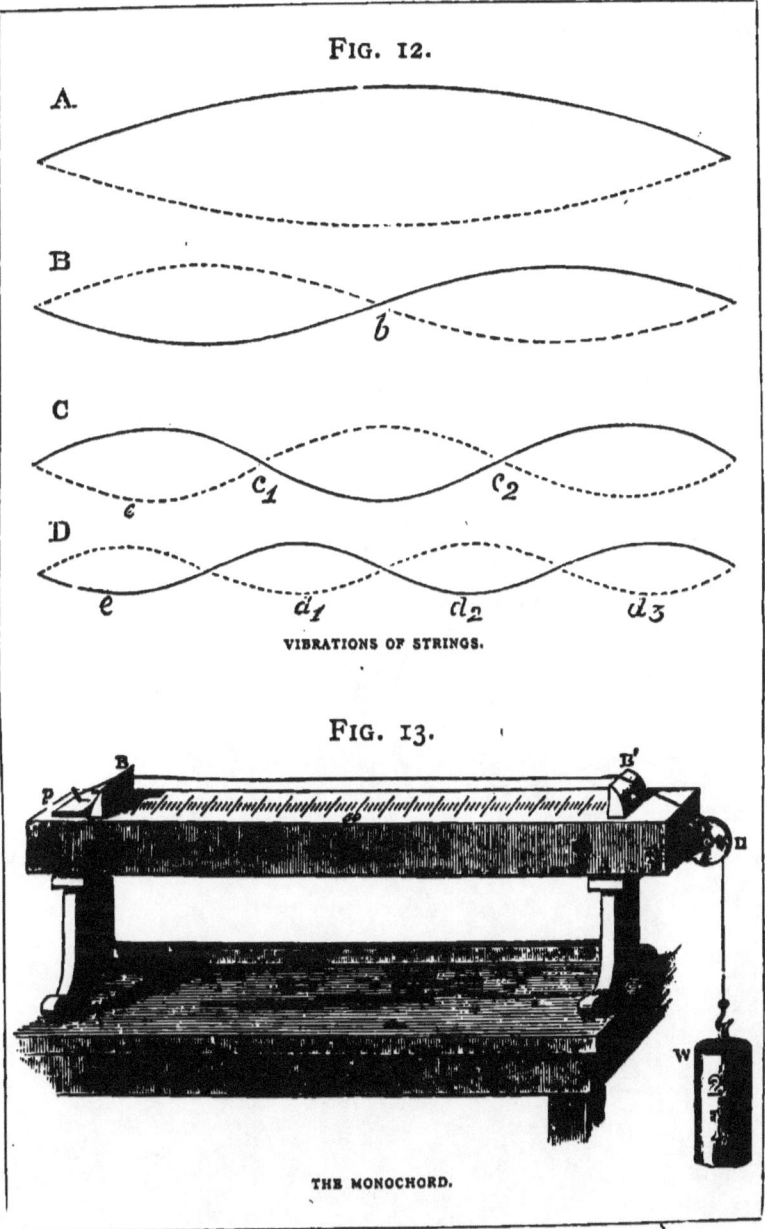

FIG. 12.

VIBRATIONS OF STRINGS.

FIG. 13.

THE MONOCHORD.

dead tone will be produced unless a nodal point has been pressed against. In the latter case the harmonic tone alone will be heard.

The vibrations of strings, although extremely complex, are all divisible into the simple pendular motions that have been described in the previous chapters respecting other vibrating bodies.

In a single note of the pianoforte many harmonic or partial tones may be distinctly heard, together forming one composite note; but the simple pendulatory motion will still be found between the different nodes of this string. By means of the spectrum, white light may be separated into its component colours; and by means of the resonator,* sound may be separated into its composite tones.

The discovery of these upper partial tones is sometimes ascribed to Sauveur; but Chladni proved that Noble and Pigott had previously discovered them at Oxford in 1676.

When a string is in vibration the series of pulsations rapidly follow one another, and when these reach the bridge they return and come in opposition to those that immediately follow them. This causes the division of

---

* The resonator is a species of ear-trumpet invented by Helmholtz. This instrument enables the listener to hear one distinct note only amongst a number of complex sounds.

the string into two vibrating parts which are called *ventral segments;* and the point of rest caused by the opposing waves is termed a *node.* The first meeting of these pulsations is succeeded by that of numberless other opposing pulsations, which rapidly subdivide the string into an infinity of ventral segments, each of which has its own pendular motion. To vibrate transversely a string must be stretched between two rigid points which are usually termed *bridges.*

An extremely useful instrument called the monochord or *sonometer* (Fig. 13, p. 37) will give some interesting rules connected with the vibrations of stretched strings. From the pin *p*, to which one end of it is firmly attached, a string passes across the two bridges B and B^1, being afterwards carried over the wheel H. The string is finally stretched by a weight attached to its extremity. The bridges B and B^1, which constitute the real ends of the string, are fastened on to the sounding-box M, N. When this string is plucked in the middle it vibrates from side to side for some time, and a sound can be distinctly heard. This sound, however, does not proceed from the string, but from the box beneath, which forms a sounding-board.

The vibrations of a thin stretched string are audible at a short distance; but in the monochord the wave motion of the string is communicated through the bridge to the column of air in the box beneath, which then becomes the real sounding body. This will give some idea of the immense importance that should be attached to the sounding-board of a pianoforte. If the sounding-board be not exactly proportioned to the length and weight of the strings that it carries, the tone must inevitably suffer. The sounding-board must, therefore, be exactly fitted to take up the vibrations of the wires that pass over it. The strings of a pianoforte do not throw the surrounding air into sonorous vibration; this is done by the sounding-board to which the string is attached acting on the air inclosed by its surface. The tone of a pianoforte depends very greatly upon the quality of material, shape, and construction of its sounding-board.

To prove the use of sounding-boards, Kilburn encased a musical box in several thicknesses of felt, through which a wooden rod passed, one end resting on the box. When the musical box was played, no sound was heard until a thin board was placed against the outer end of the rod, when the sonorous motion was immediately communicated to the surrounding air.

The sounding-board of a pianoforte should be made of wood of the most perfect elasticity; for imperfectly elastic wood expends the motion imparted to it in the friction of its own molecules, and the motion is thus converted into heat, instead of sound. The upper bridge, on the wrest-plank, should be as rigid as possible, and the lower or *belly bridge* should be fixed on the most yielding portion of the sounding-board.

The sonorous quality of the wood is mellowed by age, and playing upon the instrument greatly improves the tone, as the molecules of the wood are thus compelled to conform to the requirements of the vibrating strings. A sound-wave (according to the English and German measurement) consists of the alternate condensation and rarefaction of the air: the measurement being taken from condensation to condensation, or from rarefaction to rarefaction.

Professor Stokes remarks that, although the amplitude of the vibrating board may be very small, still its larger area renders the abolition of the condensations and rarefactions difficult, as the air cannot move in front nor pass in behind, before it is sensibly condensed and rarefied. A thin string, therefore, that would be quite inaudible when vibrated alone, will be distinctly heard when placed in connection with an appropriate sounding-board.

In the monochord the exact octave to the fundamental tone is obtained by placing a bridge so that it divides the strings into two exactly equal parts, as the vibrations of the two sections are thus doubled, each half vibrating twice as rapidly as the whole. When the string is divided into three vibrating segments the rate is tripled, and the *fifth* above the octave is produced. If the strings be divided into four parts the rate of vibration will be quadrupled, and each section will produce the double octave of the entire strings. The rule for this division is: *The number of vibrations is inversely proportional to the length of the string. The numbers of vibrations of a string are proportional to the square roots of the stretching weights.* For instance, if the string in the monochord be attached to a weight of twenty-six pounds, a certain number of vibrations will be produced each second. To double this number of vibrations a weight of 104 pounds must be employed; to treble them the weight must be 234 pounds, and so on. The more tightly the string is drawn, the higher in proportion will its pitch be raised. *When the stretching weight, length, and material of strings are equal, the number of vibrations varies inversely as the thickness of the string.*

A thin string will therefore execute double the number of vibrations in the same time as one of double the diameter, if both are of the same length and are equally stretched. The vibrations of a string also depend upon the density of the matter of which it is composed, for *the number of vibrations is inversely proportional to the square root of the density of the string, if all the other conditions are the same.*

The strings of a pianoforte are in reality simply vibrating rods.

The harmonics or upper partial tones of these depend upon the stroke, the place struck, and upon the density, rigidity, and elasticity of the string. *The strength and number of the harmonics depend upon the abruptness of the discontinuities in the motion excited.* A sharply pointed hammer or other plectrum produces a shrill tone with a great number of high tinkling harmonic tones; but the fundamental tone exceeds that of any of these partial tones. Immediately after a blow has been struck by a sharp metallic hammer, the only point directly set in motion is the one struck, the remainder of the string being at rest. A wave of deflection then arises which rapidly runs backwards and forwards over the string. This limitation of the original motion to a single point produces the most abrupt discontinuities, and a corresponding long series of harmonics having intensities in most cases equalling, and sometimes even surpassing, that of the fundamental tone.

Helmholtz remarks,[*] "When the hammer is soft and elastic, the motion has time to spread before the hammer rebounds. When thus struck, the point of the

---

[*] "Sensations of Tone." By Helmholtz. 1875. P. 122.

string in contact with such a hammer is not set in motion with a jerk, but increases gradually and continuously in velocity during the contact. The discontinuity of the motion is consequently much less, diminishing as the softness of the hammer increases, and the force of the high upper partial tones is correspondingly decreased.

"We can easily convince ourselves of the correctness of these statements by opening the top of any pianoforte, and keeping one of the keys down with a weight, so as to free the string from the damper, plucking the string at pleasure with a point, and striking it with a metallic edge on the pianoforte-hammer itself. The qualities of tone thus obtained will be entirely different. When the string is struck or plucked with hard metal the tone is piercing and tinkling, and a little attention suffices to make us hear a multitude of very high partial tones.

"These disappear, and the tone of the string becomes duller, softer, and more harmonious when we pluck the string with the soft finger, or strike it with the proper soft hammer."

Pianoforte-hammers should therefore be made as firm as possible in the coverings next to the wood, and the layer of felt that immediately strikes the string should be soft and silky upon its surface, so as to prevent the harmonics from harshly overpowering the fundamental tone. The hammer has an immense influence upon the tone produced by it. Theory proves that those harmonics are especially favoured whose periodic time is nearly equal to twice the period during which the hammer lies on the string; and that, on the other hand, those disappear whose periodic time is six, ten, fourteen, &c., times as great. The place to be struck must now be considered. When the blow is struck upon a nodal point of the string, the harmonics that have a node at this point will disappear; but those partial tones that have their greatest displacement at this point will be considerably increased.

The musical tone of a string can therefore be greatly varied by changing the place at which the hammer strikes. For instance, if the string be struck exactly in the centre the octave harmonics disappear, but the third partial tones are extremely strong, for the blow is then exactly in the centre of the middle ventral segment. In this case the fourth harmonic is not heard, as the central node is then the same as the point struck—two-fourths being the central point of the string.

All the other even partials—the sixth, eighth, and so on—disappear in the same manner, producing a hollow quality of tone. When the string is struck at one-third of its length, those harmonics that have an odd number—the third, sixth, and ninth—are not heard, and the result is slightly better than when the string is struck in the middle. If the string is struck near its end, the upper harmonics are greatly strengthened, and a thin quality of tone is thus produced.

When the point of excitement is between the seventh and ninth of the entire length, the seventh and ninth harmonics become weak, and they are then almost inaudible. This, by experience, has been found to be the best place to give the blow. In the extreme treble the shortness and rigidity of the strings preclude the possibility of the production of audible harmonics, and it is therefore usual to strike higher in the treble than in the tenor and bass, for the purpose of rendering the treble brilliant.

For the longer strings the upper harmonics would be too loud and tinkling if a higher point than the ninth were struck, as the fundamental tone would be partly overpowered by them. On the other hand, the nearer the string is struck in its middle the duller and more hollow will its tone become, as the fundamental tone will then greatly outweigh the harmonics. The same effect may also be produced with a heavy and soft hammer, without altering the striking place. Indeed, the point of striking so greatly depends upon other causes, which will be considered in the ensuing chapters, that theory alone is generally inaccurate when it names the exact point for producing the tone best suited to the taste of a cultivated musician.

In Germany and America the seventh is the striking point usually chosen, and a heavy hammer is almost invariably used. The result is that a heavy, hollow quality of tone is produced.

In France, where the musical instruments are always metallic and bright in tone, the striking point is one-eighth of the entire length.

The faults of these two systems are that the German and American tone usually becomes dull and heavy, and the French tone soon wears hard and harsh. In the first instance the soft felt on the hammers quickly cuts, and clings round the string after the blow has been given; and in the second the upper harmonics are disagreeably perceptible when the hammers have become slightly worn.

The thickness and material of the strings also have a great influence upon the tone produced by them. When the instrument is heavily strung the rigidity of the strings will preclude the very high harmonics from being heard, as they cannot vibrate between two nodes that are very near each other. These upper harmonic tones are extremely close together, being less than a whole tone apart in the eighth and upper partial tones;

and the interval is less than a semitone in the fifteenth and upwards. These tones are consequently dissonant. The piano should therefore be strung sufficiently heavily to prevent the highest harmonics from being heard at all.

To sum up the matter of harmonics it may be added that *a string vibrates as a whole, with a pendular motion between the two nodal points of its two bridges.* In addition to this simple motion, it can also form smaller vibrating segments, called *ventral segments*, each of which also has this separate pendular motion, and is divided from the next ventral segment by a node, which is a point of partial rest. This subdivision into a larger or smaller number of ventral segments, whose vibrations produce the harmonics or partial tones of the string and the intervals between these harmonics, constitute what is known in Great Britain as *quality of tone*, in France *timbre*, and in Germany as *Klangfarbe*.

It is this union of high and low tones which enables a musician to distinguish one musical instrument from another. For instance, the tones of a harp or of a guitar are not confounded with those of a pianoforte; for the catgut strings do not produce such high harmonic sounds as those caused by the wire strings of a pianoforte.

A hard hammer and a light string are favourable to the production of high overtones; and a heavy string and a soft hammer sound the fundamental note so plainly that these high partial tones almost entirely disappear. They also depend to a great extent upon the rapidity with which the hammer leaves the string after the impact has taken place, and upon the point at which the blow is delivered.

Helmholtz found that if the fundamental tone were called 100, the second harmonic was 56·1 when twanged with the finger; but when the same string was struck with a pianoforte-hammer, whose contact with the string endured for three-sevenths of the period of vibration of the fundamental tone, the intensity of the same tone was nine, and the second overtone was almost inaudible. When, however, the duration of contact was diminished to three-twentieths of the period of the fundamental tone, the intensity of the harmonic rose to 357; and when a hard hammer was used, and the blow sharply delivered, the intensity obtained was 505, or more than five times the number of the primary tone.

These effects have been plainly shown by the experiments of the Brothers Weber, who made them visible in various ways, one of which was the use of thin black cords in front of white paper.

Of the longitudinal vibrations of wires by means of resined rubbers it is not necessary to speak, as this system of vibration has not yet been introduced into the pianoforte.

Experiments with Dove's polyphonic sirene prove that two rows of an equal number of holes produce the same pitch as each other when blown into, whether one set of holes be larger or smaller than the other row, if they revolve with equal velocity. When the rate of rotation is doubled, the pitch of the note is raised an octave higher. For instance, if a revolving disc be perforated with one row of twenty holes and another row of ten holes, the sounds produced will be those of a note and its octave, as double the number of vibrations are given by the larger series of holes when wind is blown through them during their rotation. It is therefore proved that a musical tone which is an octave higher than another makes exactly twice as many vibrations in a given time as the latter. When the number of holes is respectively eight and twelve a note and its fifth are produced, regardless of the rate at which the disc revolves. The fifth therefore is formed when the vibrations that form the higher sound are three in the same time as two of the lower tone. Dove's polyphonic sirene usually has four series of holes—eight, ten, twelve, and sixteen respectively.

By means of this instrument and by other experiments it has been proved that the relation of vibrational numbers are the octave as 1 : 2; the fifth, 2 : 3; the fourth, 3 : 4; the major third, 4 : 5; and the minor third, 5 : 6.

These differences of relation may be easily understood if we remember that in a *unison* the two strings vibrate exactly the same number of times per second. Thus the vibrations of one string sounding in unison with another are as the number 1 : 1. When the octave string is sounded its vibrations are exactly twice that number, therefore they are as the numbers 2 : 1; that is to say, in an octave the higher note is produced by exactly twice the number of vibrations per second that produce the lower note. When two vibrations of the one note fall upon the ear in precisely the same time as three vibrations of another note, these two sounds produce the interval of a *fifth;* the relation being 2 : 3, and so on with the other intervals.

Helmholtz says,* "When the fundamental tone of a given interval is taken an octave higher, the interval is said to be inverted. Thus a fourth is an inverted fifth, a minor sixth an inverted major third, and a major sixth an inverted minor third. The corresponding ratios of the vibrational numbers are consequently

---

* "Sensations of Tone." By Herman C. J. Helmholtz. 1875. P. 22.

obtained by doubling the smaller number in the original interval."

From 2 : 3, the fifth, we thus have   3 : 4, the fourth.
„   4 : 5, the major third ,,   5 : 8, the minor sixth.
„   5 : 6, the minor third, 6 : 10, = 3 : 5, the major sixth.

These are all the consonant intervals which lie within the compass of an octave. With the exception of the minor sixth, which is really the most imperfect of the aobve consonances, the ratios of their vibrational numbers are all expressed by means of the whole numbers, 1, 2, 3, 4, 5, 6.

Comparatively simple and easy experiments with the sirene corroborate the remarkable law that *the vibrational numbers of consonant musical tones bear to each other ratios expressible by small whole numbers.*

The same law, of course, governs the length and vibrations of strings. Thus, if the string of a monochord be divided into two parts by a bridge in such a manner that two-thirds of the length lie to the right and one-third to the left, so that the two lengths are in the ratio of 2 : 1 they give the interval of an octave, the greater length giving the deeper tone. When the bridge is so placed that three-fifths of the string lie to the right and two-fifths to the left, the ratio of the two lengths is 3 : 2, and the interval is a fifth. In a seven

E

and a quarter octave pianoforte the vibrations of the lowest bass note A are about twenty-seven and a half each second, and those of the extreme treble note C^v are 4,224 per second.

The notes of the lowest octave are not plainly discernible to ordinary auditors, but the treble notes may be extended to nearly three and a half extra octaves before they will pass beyond the reach of musical hearing. This is very wonderful if it be remembered that, to produce this sense of hearing an extreme treble note, the tympanum of the ear vibrates 38,000 times in a second of time, and it shows what a great variety of different vibrational numbers can be perceived and distinguished by the ear. In this respect the ear is far superior to the eye (which distinguishes light of different periods of vibrations by the sensation of different colours); for the compass of the vibrations of light distinguishable by the eye little exceeds an octave.

The periodic time* of the vibration of a string determines the *pitch* of the note produced; the amplitude of this vibration determines the power of the note; and in general terms it may be said that the *quality of the tone* produced depends upon the form of vibration of the string. Every different quality of tone requires a

---

* Appendix B, p. 189.

different form of vibration, although different forms of vibration may correspond to the same quality of tone. For example, the violin-piano, when played in the same manner as an harmonium, produces the same quality of tone as a reedy instrument of that class, the harmonics being almost identically the same, although the form of vibration of the string in the violin-piano is entirely dissimilar to that of the reed in the harmonium.

PART II.

CHAPTER IV.

THE HISTORY OF MUSIC.

IT may be interesting, in tracing the history of the pianoforte, to give some slight account of the rise and progress of its parent and offspring, Music; for the advance of music and the development of musical instruments have always been simultaneous, the one greatly influencing the other. Indeed, the chronicles of "the drawing-room orchestra" are almost indissolubly linked with those of music. The universe itself is considered by modern as well as ancient philosophers to be formed upon principles of harmony, and this idea is not confined to such philosophers as Isaac Newton, for the greatest poets favour this theory. Shakespeare beautifully expresses the idea in the well-known lines—

> There's not the smallest orb that thou behold'st,
> But in his motion like an angel sings,
> Still quiring to the young-eyed cherubims;
> Such harmony is in immortal sounds!
> But whilst this muddy vesture of decay
> Doth grossly close us in we cannot hear it.

Burney says, "Harmony being part of nature, we cannot speak of any *inventor* of music. The first attempts must have been rude and artless; the first flute a whistling reed, in imitation of the wind as it blew along the living reeds; and the primitive lyre, perhaps, the dried sinews of some animal."

It is not easy to determine who the first cultivators of music were, but as all ancient histories speak of the grandeur and civilisation of Egypt, at a time when Phrygia and other musical nations were in a comparatively rude state, it is probable that Egypt was the first nation to bring to any degree of perfection the instruments of music handed down to them by the descendants of Jubal, who "was the father [or chief] of all such as handle the harp [or lyre] and [mouth] organ."

It would be useless to attempt to trace music to a higher source than Egypt, for even in the time of Abram the Egyptians were formed into a nation with a king at its head; and the earlier references to the art are so purely incidental that they give us little clue to the amount of knowledge of instrumental music previously acquired.

In the antediluvian world, Jubal, we are told by the Scriptures, was a player on both wind and stringed instruments; the harp, or lyre rather, and the syrinx being expressly mentioned. It appears also that the art of music was cultivated in Mesopotamia, and that it was used upon festive occasions. The enraged Laban, in reproaching his son-in-law Jacob for leaving secretly to return to his own country, indignantly says, "I might have sent thee away with mirth and with songs, with tabret [tambourine] and with harp." The next reference shows an advance in vocal music, which, in true Asiatic style, was probably performed in unison with the accompanying instruments, and generally in combination with poetry and dancing. Miriam in her jubilant outburst—" Sing ye to the Lord, for he hath triumphed gloriously; the horse and his rider hath he thrown into the sea "—" took a timbrel in her hand; and all the women went out after her with timbrels and with dances. And Miriam *answered* [that is, *sang responsively to*] Moses and the men of Israel." This is the first mention we have of any advance in music, and it was really a great advance; for *antiphonal* singing, the one part answering to the other, would naturally lead on to counterpoint and harmony.

This incident, it will be remembered, occurred after the liberated Hebrews left Egpyt; and it is therefore only natural to conjecture that they had made this improvement in their music during their stay in that country, for we can perceive by monumental evidence that music was cultivated there long previously to that time. Besides, the Greeks, who lost no merit by neglecting to claim it, unanimously confessed that most of the ancient musical instruments were of Egyptian invention.

The changes in government, manners, and amusements, caused by the country being successively conquered, after the reigns of the Pharaohs, by the Ethiopians, Persians, Greeks, and Romans, were great, so that music did not make uniform progress in Egypt. The ancient Egyptian account of the introduction of the first musical instrument is that the mythical Hermes (who was supposed to have lived between the years 1800 and 1500 B.C., and was afterwards deified for his genius and services as the great secretary of the celebrated king and sun-god Osiris) was walking along the sunny banks of the Nile, when he struck his foot against the shell of a tortoise. The flesh being wasted and dried, nothing was left within the shell but nerves and cartilages. These, being braced and contracted by desiccation, produced so pleasant a sound that it suggested the first idea of a lyre to him; and he afterwards constructed a musical instrument in the form of a tortoise, stringing it with the dried sinews of dead animals. This fable has been repeated in many countries, even Ireland having a very similar legend. But although the idea is pretty, the story can scarcely be considered as trustworthy.

That the Egyptian lyre and harp rapidly improved is shown by the discoveries of Bruce and other great travellers of most perfect instruments drawn upon tombs and monuments. It is therefore a matter of wonder that, many years afterwards, other instruments of inferior kinds and with fewer strings should take their place. In music, as in everything else, there seems a boundary set; and, like the stone of Sisyphus, when one arrives at it he is precipitated back to the level whence he started, and the work has to be begun afresh. It seems to admit of but little doubt that the Egyptians had, in the most flourishing times of their empire, music and musical instruments which were far superior to those of other countries; but after their subjection to the Persians this music and these instruments were lost, and not regained until the time of the Ptolemies, when music, together with the other arts, was encouraged at the court of Alexandria more than at any other place in the known world, till the captivity of

Cleopatra, an event which terminated both the empire and history of the Egyptians.

Of the Egyptian system of notation nothing can be said, for ancient writings, although they often hint at it, never give any description. It seems probable, however, that their music was expressed by their alphabet, like that of other ancient nations.

As the music of the Assyrians was probably very similar to that of the Egyptians, it will not call for any particular remark.

The Hebrews, having derived improvements in music from the Egyptians, many imitations of their instruments would naturally be made in a modified form to adapt them to the long Israelitish wanderings. Moses, learned as he was " in all the wisdom of the Egyptians," would not fail to instruct the people under his charge in the musical praises of God.

After this, Samuel formed schools where the prophets were instructed in music, with which they were accustomed to soothe their own angry moods, and produce a fit state of mind for receiving the gift of prophecy. David was trained at these schools, and the power of the music he produced, in calming Saul's troubled and moody mind, proves that music in David's time had again arrived at comparative perfection.

The musical services of the Jewish Temple were on

an extraordinarily grand scale, and of an extremely noisy description. If we may give credence to Josephus, who is often inaccurate when speaking of music, there were two hundred thousand trumpets and forty thousand other instruments of music with which to praise God at the dedication of Solomon's Temple.

Grecian music is said to have originated at the birth of Jupiter, when Rhea, his mother, appointed the Curetes to nurse and teach him. These danced about him in armour with great noise, that Saturn, his father, might not hear him cry:—

> These represent the armèd priests who strove
> To drown the tender cries of infant Jove;
> By dancing quick they made a greater sound,
> And beat their armour as they danced around.
> CREECH.

After this rude, warlike music, drums and cymbals were the first Grecian instruments of percussion; and having but one tone, required little art in the player.

The Greeks, as the Egyptians and Hebrews had probably done before them, used their alphabetical characters for symbols of sound; but finding twenty-four insufficient to express the sounds in their three genera, Diatonic, Chromatic, and Enharmonic, they transposed the letters, sometimes placing them horizontally, making some large, and some small, and mutilating and altering them so as to increase their symbolic power. As the scale extended these characters increased, for marks of accent were added, until at last, according to Buretti's calculation, the enormous number of sixteen hundred and twenty characters were employed.

In the time of Aristoxenus (341 B.C.), the oldest writer upon music whose works have been preserved, the Greek system was called *Systema perfectum, maximum, immutatum*—the great, the perfect, the immutable system; but perhaps modern musicians may not be so enthusiastic respecting a notation that appears to be as perfect a muddle as any classical nation ever tolerated.

Ancient authors tell us that the Greeks, in writing their music, placed two rows of characters over the words of a lyric poem, the upper row serving for the voice, and the lower for the instruments. The multiplicity of these characters must certainly have made music in ancient Greece a long and laborious study. It is not therefore surprising that Plato, although he was unwilling that youth should bestow too much time upon music, allowed them three years to learn the rudiments.

Despite these disadvantages, music made great progress in Greece; indeed, modern European music is directly derived from it.

The Roman music was derived from the Etruscan,

and was exceedingly rough, until the Romans in the Augustine age borrowed the musical instruments and music of the Greeks, when it received an impetus that is still felt; as it awakened a love of music which now seems inborn in Italians.

Music having been used by the Egyptians, Hebrews, Greeks, and Romans, in their religious ceremonies, it is not surprising that the early Christians were particularly partial to singing psalms and hymns—singing even in prison and on the point of martyrdom. Their music, however, does not seem to have been of any new species; and it is probable that the music of the period, and perhaps even pagan hymn-tunes, were adopted. The use of music was universal amongst the early Christians long before they had built any churches, or their religion had been recognised by law as the established religion of the Roman empire (A.D. 312). In 313 Constantine built many sumptuous churches, in which music formed a very important part of the ceremonies. During the reign of Theodosius the Ambrosian chant was established in the church of Milan, and the psalms and hymns were exceedingly beautiful. The performance was so good that the Gentiles, who went from curiosity, often liked the service so well that they were baptised before leaving. After this, music was even more carefully practised in the Church, and

Pope Gregory the Great, in the year 590, collected and arranged the hymns and psalms that had been used by the primitive Christians. This arrangement, called the Antiphònarium Centonem, was long in vogue at Rome, and was soon adopted in the Western Church, where the Gregorian chants are still great favourites.

From the time of Pope Gregory to that of Guido there was no other distinction of key than that of authentic and plagal; nor were there any semitones used but those from E to F, B to C, and occasionally A to B.

The musical notation was precisely the same in the Christian Church as that of the ancient Greeks, the Greek appellatives for the musical scale being used in the time of Boethius in 526. Pope Gregory used the first seven of the Roman letters in such a way that they stood for three octaves, thus: A, B, C, D, E, F, G, signified one octave; *a, b, c, d, e, f, g*, the octave above; aa, bb, cc, dd, ee, ff, gg, the octave again; so that three octaves were symbolised by these seven letters, which are still retained in most parts of Europe, although a different *entablature* and a new *notation* are used in practice, and seem destined to become universal. After the Greek characters were disused, many systems of notation were introduced; but, for a long time, none were so popular as that of Pope Gregory. The other musical signs and notes were most difficult to understand, and an ancient writer, speaking of them, said, "These irregular signs must be productive of more error than science, as they are often so carelessly and promiscuously placed that, while one was singing a semitone or a fourth, another would sing a third or a fifth." About the year 1022, Guido Aretinus, a Benedictine monk at Arezzo in Tuscany, who was employed in correcting the ecclesiastical chants, composed a scale conformable to the Greek system, adding a few notes to it above and below. Discovering afterwards that the first syllable of each hemistich in the hymn to St. John the Baptist formed a regular series of six sounds ascending—*Ut, re, mi, fa, sol, la*—he placed at the sides of each of these syllables one of the first seven letters of the alphabet, A, B, C, D, E, F, G; and because he accompanied the note which he added below the ancient system with the letter *gamma*, the new scale was called *gamut*, by which name it is still known. The hymn which supplied the syllables *ut, re, mi*, &c., was used at church, and begins—

> *Ut* queant laxis *re*sonare fibris,
> *Mi*ra gestorum *fa*muri tuorum,
> *Sol*ve polluti *la*bii reatum,
>   Sancti Johannis!

Guido was not only the inventor of this celebrated gamut, but is also generally considered to have been the inventor of counterpoint as well as of the organ keyboard, which was afterwards introduced into the clavichord and other instruments of the pianoforte class.

In the year 1055 Magister Franco, of Cologne, made his important invention of the musical *time-table*. This was of very great value; for time, in music, can impart meaning and energy to the repetition of the same note. For nearly two centuries after Guido's arrangement of the scale, and Franco's invention of the time-table, no remains of secular music can be discovered, except those of the Troubadours.

In the thirteenth century melody seems to have been little more than plain-song or chanting. The notes were square, and written on four lines only, in the C clef, and it was not until the end of the reign of St. Louis (in 1269) that the fifth line was added to the stave.

Music then made rapid progress, although principally in the Church, until the sixteenth century, when madrigals and fantasias were introduced in Italy.

The three modern schools of music—the German, Italian, and French—have originated those great musical forms, the sonata, the symphony, and the opera. The present German school was founded and built up by Handel, Bach, Haydn, Mozart. Beethoven,

Wagner and Brahms, who gave an entirely new, intellectual, and really artistic character to music, by employing in their compositions subjects appropriate to the character intended in the particular piece, and by treating the different elements of musical pleasure in a methodical and artistic manner. These composers have raised the German school far above the two others; for not only have they produced sonatas and symphonies which are at present unapproachable, but in opera and oratorio also their masterpieces reign supreme, the light and pretty music of the Italian and French schools being immeasurably below this standard of excellence.

That the English have no school of music, properly so called, appears extraordinary when it is considered that in the peculiarly English ballads and glees there are such excellent materials to commence with. Our composers seem content to imitate the German, and occasionally the French and Italian schools; still, it is to be hoped that the time is not far distant when England will boast a school of music that may be properly claimed as her own.

CHAPTER V.

STRINGED MUSICAL INSTRUMENTS OF THE ANCIENTS.

SEVERAL instruments of the ancients have been mentioned to which the pianoforte owes its origin. In sketching the birth and development of this instrument it will be necessary to give some short description of these its ancestors. Much light has been thrown on the subject by various interesting researches and discoveries made in the present century; for not only have we learned much of ancient musical instruments from the sculptures and paintings that have been discovered, but several of the instruments themselves have been found in tombs or other protected places, where they had remained silent beside their buried masters an extraordinarily long time, almost without change. One—an Egyptian harp—was found in an ancient tomb at Thebes, and when the catgut strings upon it were touched the harp still emitted sounds, although it had been unused probably for three thousand years. In describing these ancient instruments it will be necessary to name those only from which the pianoforte has immediately descended.

Amongst ancient stringed instruments, the harp and lyre are probably of the greatest antiquity, but which of these can claim priority of invention it is impossible to discover with certainty. The harps, which were much used in ancient Egypt and Assyria, varied greatly in size and shape, as will be seen from the illustrations of Egyptian harps, Fig. 14, p. 71.

Those made for single use were portable and light, while those for choral accompaniments were large and powerful, being evidently intended to stand on the ground. Carl Engel, in "The Music of the Most Ancient Nations," remarks that "the Asiatic harps never had a front pillar to assist in withstanding the tension on the strings, as we have in our own; but probably metal or ivory was used in the manufacture, to permit of the strings being screwed up very tightly." The harp of the Burmese and other inhabitants of the countries situated between Hindoostan and China is very similar to the Assyrian. The Burmese harp is tuned by tasselled cords at the end of the strings, which are bound to the upper curved end so that they can be pushed up or down in tuning the instrument. This is similar to the manner occasionally adopted by

FIG. 14.

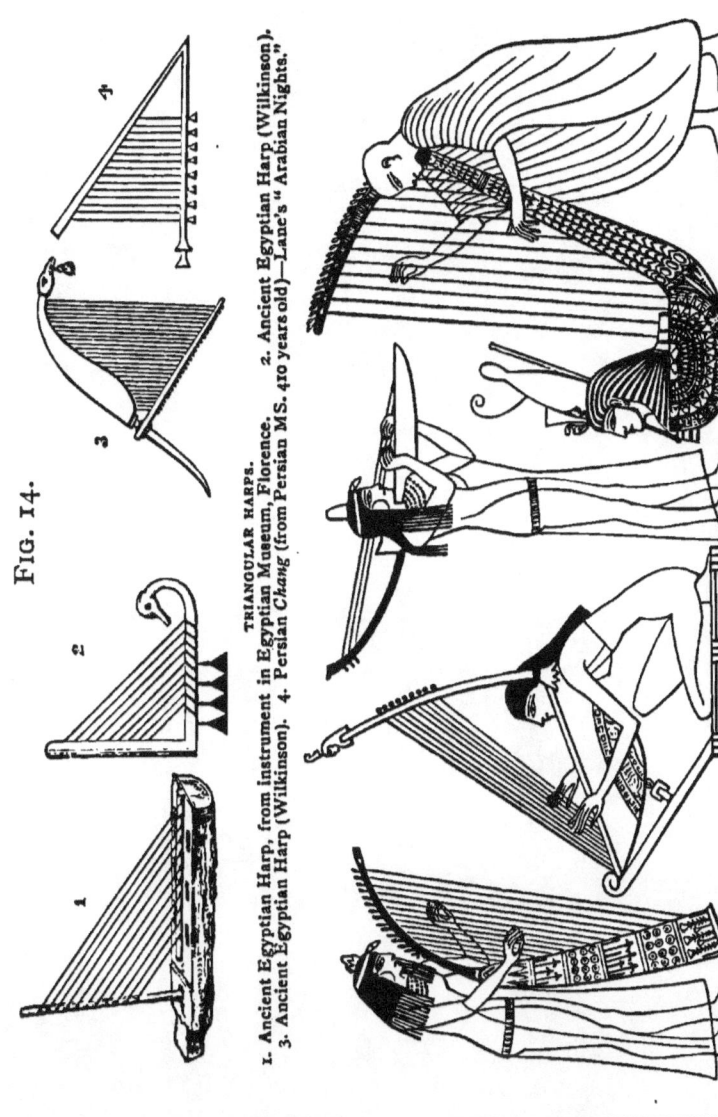

TRIANGULAR HARPS.

1. Ancient Egyptian Harp, from instrument in Egyptian Museum, Florence. 2. Ancient Egyptian Harp (Wilkinson). 3. Ancient Egyptian Harp (Wilkinson). 4. Persian *Chang* (from Persian MS. 410 years old)—Lane's "Arabian Nights."

VARIOUS FORMS OF EGYPTIAN HARPS (ROSELLINI).

1 and 3. Portable Harps for single use. 2. Orchestral Harp. 4. From Painting at Thebes, on tomb of Rameses III.

F 2

the ancients; but their usual system of tuning seems to have been by tuning-pegs, round which the strings were passed.

The Egyptian harps were sometimes most remarkable for elegance of form and elaborate decoration. The celebrated traveller James Bruce found two, painted in fresco, on the wall of an ancient sepulchre at Thebes, which is supposed to be that of Rameses III., who reigned about 1250 B.C. Dr. Burney, in his "History of Music," published Bruce's letter to him, accompanied by drawings of one of these harps.

The discovery of these drawings created a great sensation, and was hardly believed until confirmed by other travellers. Bruce, with much truth, says, "These harps, in my opinion, overturn all the accounts hitherto given of the earliest state of ancient musical instruments in the East, and are altogether, in their form, ornament, and compass, an incontestable proof that geometry, drawing, mechanics, and music were at the greatest perfection when this instrument was made, and that the period from which we date the invention of these arts was only the beginning of the era of their restoration. . . . One of these harps has thirteen strings, but wants the fore-piece of the frame opposite to the longest string. The back part is the sounding-board, composed of four thin pieces of wood joined together in form of a cone—that is, growing wider towards the bottom; so that as the length of the string increases, the square of the corresponding space in the sounding-board, in which the sound was to undulate, always increases in proportion. The whole of the principles on which this harp are constructed are rational and ingenious, and the ornamental parts are executed in the very best manner. It would be impossible even now either to construct or to finish a harp of any form with more taste or elegance." But harps of this description, having no front pillar, could not be heavily strung, nor would they stand well in tune.

The lyre, which is perhaps even more than the harp the immediate ancestor of the pianoforte, was much used in Egypt and Assyria, especially for religious festivities. The illustrations on p. 75; Fig. 15, will convey some idea of the shape of these ancient lyres, and the manner in which they were played.

The drawings of the first two Assyrian lyres are from sculptures found at Konyunjik, and now in the British Museum; the third is taken from Botta's "Ninève."

It will be noticed that the lyres were of many different shapes, and that the strings being partly carried, as in the pianoforte, over the sounding-board, were not free to be struck upon both sides throughout their entire length by the plectra or by the fingers of the performer.

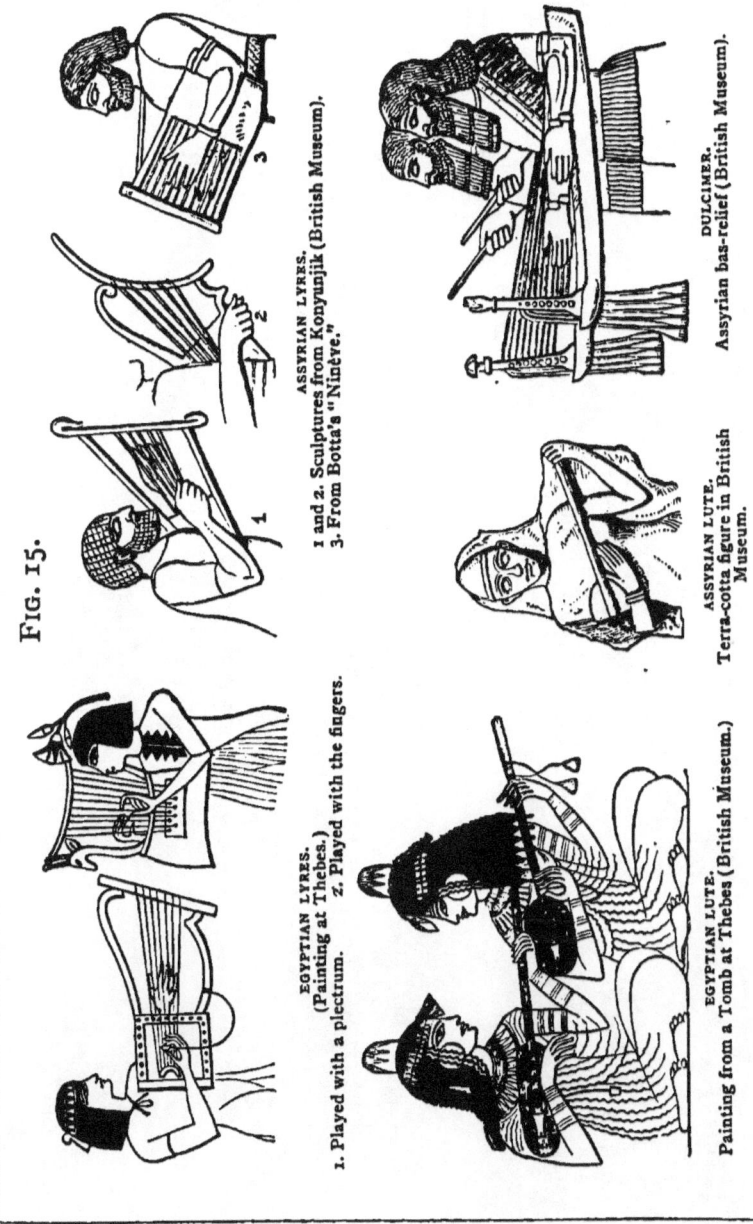

This is the distinction between the harp and the lyre, for the harp can be played the whole length of the strings upon both sides, as the sounding-board is differently placed. Both instruments were played with the fingers, and the lyre with the *plectrum* also, which was generally a small piece of ivory or bone, (as in illustration 1, on p. 75,) *pressed* by the player against the strings, and snapping them as though they were pulled by the finger. The Irish, however, with their usual originality, allowed their finger-nails to grow so long that they were enabled to employ them as natural plectra.

The plectra were sometimes short wands or sticks, similar to that used by the player on the dulcimer in illustration 16, p. 79, and in the representation of the Assyrian dulcimer in Fig. 15, p. 75. They were held one in each hand, and were used for *striking* the strings of the instrument played upon, so as o set them in vibration. The first kind of plectrum suggested the crow-quill that snapped the strings in the spinet and harpsichord; the second probably gave the idea of the hammer for striking the strings in the pianoforte, as the plectrum of wood was after some time covered on one side with leather, so that the performer could play softly by striking the strings with the part covered with leather or loudly by using the wooden side. This was succeeded by the dulcimer hammers, from which those of the pianoforte are evidently borrowed.

The Egyptian as well as the Assyrian lyres varied greatly in shape and number of strings. Two of these instruments, one in the Leyden Museum and the other in the Berlin Museum, are still in a remarkably perfect state of preservation. They are made entirely of wood, and, as in the Assyrian lyres, the frames are longer on one side than on the other, for the purpose of tuning the strings by sliding them up to sharpen, or down to flatten them. The lyre was a very favourite instrument with the Greeks, and was probably imported by them from Egypt through Asia Minor.

Perhaps the dulcimer, even more than the harp and lyre, was the immediate ancestor of the pianoforte. It was played with the plectrum for *striking*, both by the Egyptians and Assyrians, and, later, by the Hebrews and Persians, The strings in this instrument passed completely over the sounding-board, and were of varying lengths. The Assyrian dulcimer is represented in Fig. 15, p. 75, and in the illustration Fig. 16, p. 79, which are taken from a bas-relief in the British Museum, representing a procession greeting the conquerors after the victory of Sardanapalus over the Susians.

The first figure in illustration Fig. 15, p. 75, is

FIG. 16.

PART OF ASSYRIAN PROCESSION GREETING THE CONQUERORS.—(*Bas-relief*, British Museum.)
1 and 4, Assyrian Harps.   2, Double Pipes.   3, Assyrian Dulcimer.   Followers clapping hands in time.

playing the Assyrian harp; the second, has the double pipe or flute; and the third is the performer on the dulcimer. In his right hand the plectrum is held firmly, and is about to strike the strings. From the manner in which the strings run in this dulcimer, it is evident that they must have passed *over a bridge* before they took a vertical direction, but this has been very imperfectly represented. The dulcimer was generally fastened round the waist or shoulder of the performer by a strap, for convenience in playing whilst marching. As the strings run out in a straight line from the player in the same manner as in the grand piano, instead of across, as in the modern dulcimer, the player must have struck the string sideways with the plectrum, probably twanging an accompaniment upon the strings with his left hand. The dulcimer has been a favourite instrument for ages, and is still used in the East, especially by the Arabs and Persians, under the name of the *kanoon*, in which the lamb's-gut strings are twanged with two small plectra, one of which is attached to the forefinger of each hand. On the Continent, too, the dulcimer is often met with at the rural fêtes, under the name of the *Hackbrett* (*i.e.*, chopping-board), which it resembles in shape. It is a square box about four feet in length and eighteen inches in breadth, containing the sounding-board and three octaves of strings, two or three to each note, tuned in unison. The player holds a short stick in either hand, with round knobs at the end, one side of which is covered with soft leather or felt, for use in *piano* passages. The sound is pleasing when played piano, but as there are no dampers like those used in the pianoforte, and as the hand can only be used occasionally instead of them, the forte passages are very confused.

Besides the instruments mentioned, the Egyptians and Assyrians had one bearing a close resemblance to the tamboura in common use upon the shores of the Euphrates and Tigris, which has *wire* strings passing over the sounding-board of a lute-shaped instrument, and is usually played with a plectrum of tortoise-shell, or of an eagle or vulture quill. The neck and fingerboard in this instrument are remarkably long and straight, being formed of a single straight bar. Some elegant specimens of the tamboura were sent to the International Exhibition of 1862 from Turkey. This will probably explain the Assyrian instrument accurately, although the only two specimens discovered are so much defaced as to render description and comparison difficult and uncertain. There is also a representation of an Egyptian musical instrument resembling the tamboura on the *Guglia Rotta* at Rome, which has the neck, keyboard, and body well marked. This instrument alone would prove that the effeminate Egyptians and the sturdy Assyrians had made considerable advance in music at a very early age, for it shows that they knew how to produce a greater number of notes upon a few strings, by means of the finger-board, than could be obtained from their harps. There are also two or three drawings (which will be found in Fig. 16, p. 79) of this instrument in the British Museum, in which the finger-board is clearly shown, especially one on a beautifully modelled and well-preserved vase in terra-cotta, which Dr. Birch describes as " probably the oldest of all Egyptian pottery."

Besides these stringed instruments the ancients had a three-sided harp, or, rather, a harp of two sides with the last string appearing to form a third, which was called the trigonon, in addition to several other shapes of the harp and lyre, which are represented in the illustrations, Fig. 14, p. 71.

It is unnecessary to describe these successive modifications, as they were principally changes in shape only, were comparatively slight, and have little bearing upon the History of the Pianoforte. But it is interesting to notice that the systrum, a little metal instrument about eight inches in length, had thick *metal* strings passing through it, which produced a sharp ringing sound when shaken in the hand of the performer.

CHAPTER VI.

THE FIRST INSTRUMENTS WITH THE PIANOFORTE KEYBOARD —THE CLAVICYTHERIUM, CLAVICHORD, VIRGINAL, SPINET, HARPSICHORD, ETC.

It is worthy of notice how directly every musical instrument that has been considered peculiarly European appears to have been derived from the ancient Asiatic instruments. The only exception to this, perhaps, is the pianoforte, which, although merely a development of the dulcimer, played with leather-covered plectra, is converted into a new, although not original, instrument, by the addition of the finger-keys and action. This development of the lyre and dulcimer into the pianoforte, by the introduction of finger-keys, for raising many plectra at the same time, is of quite recent date, unless there were ancient instruments of a different class to those already discovered. It seems almost incredible that two thousand years should have elapsed before so natural an improvement was introduced, and yet such appears to be the fact. The first keyed instrument was the tamboura, but the first with *finger-keys* was the organ, to which, it is said, Guido applied them. These keys were like the pedals now used in organs, but with divisions only of tones, as the semitones were not used until about the year 950, when they were introduced in Venice, at which place Bernhard, a German, first made organ-pedals, or foot-keys, in 1470. Although Guido is generally considered to have been the inventor, the date of the introduction of finger-keys cannot be ascertained with certainty, for the earliest reliable mention of them is in 757 A.D., when Constantine V. sent an organ having finger-keys to Pepin, King of France, with other valuable presents. These keys were at first very similar to the *carillons* of the Netherlands, being four or five inches in width, and being struck with the clenched fist.

The next instrument with finger-keys was probably the clavicytherium, or clavitherum, as it is sometimes termed, which was introduced about the year 1300 by the Italians, and soon imitated in Belgium and Germany. The introduction of this instrument was probably due to the want felt by composers of some instrument which would give, however imperfectly, the effect of an orchestra. A kind of harp or lyre, of an oblong shape, with catgut strings arranged in the form of a half-triangle, was therefore introduced, in which the organ-keys were employed to raise the hard leather plectra for snapping the strings. It was at first in an upright position, and Sir John Hawkins says that it was brought out as a new invention long afterwards under the name of the "upright harpsichord." Subsequently this clavicytherium, or keyed cithara, was placed upon supports in a horizontal position.

Another instrument, deriving its name from employing the key (*clavis*), was the clavichord, which was in use before, or at the same time as, the clavicytherium, from which it differed, however, both in construction and in the manner of producing the tone, the strings being of wire, and set in motion by striking and pressing instead of the twanging of the leather plectrum. This striking upon the string was effected by a piece of brass in the shape of a wedge, termed the *tangent*, which was placed at the end of the key, farthest from the player, in an upright position, just under the part of the string it was to strike.

It will be seen by the drawing of the clavichord mechanism (Fig. 17, p. 87) that after the key had been pressed down and the brass wedge had struck the string, it still pressed up against it as long as the finger held the key down, raising the string up

FIG. 17.

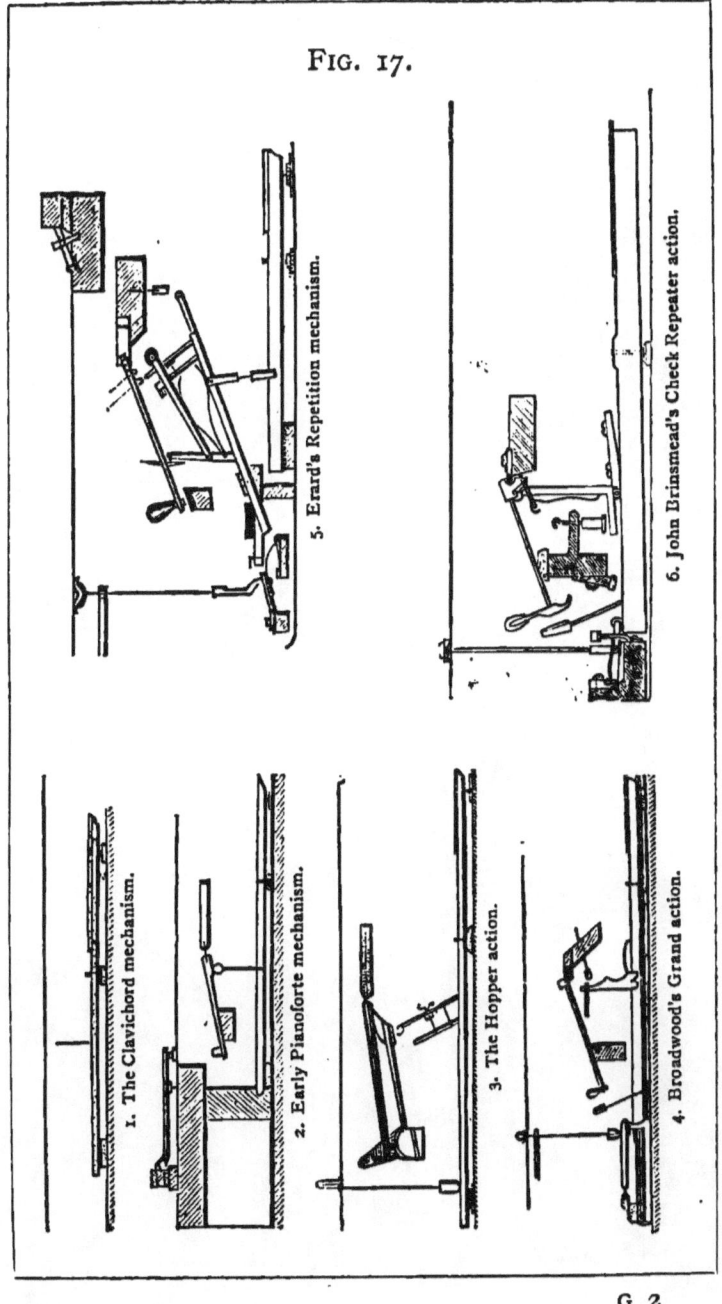

at that point. Thus dividing it, this tangent formed a second bridge over which the string passed. To prevent the string vibrating on both sides of this bridge, the shorter length had either a small piece of cloth for a damper, or else a strip of list, drawn over and under each string, which stopped the vibration of the whole length directly the finger was raised from the key. At first two notes were produced from the same string by these tangents striking and stopping the string as a violin-player's finger stops the note in different parts, producing varying lengths. It is worthy of notice that such a player as the great Sebastian Bach preferred an instrument with so feeble a tone to any other for private practice; but most excellent effects could be produced from it by an expert performer with a light touch. The staccato passages could be well rendered, and by pressing down the key after the blow had been struck the tangent could be made to still further raise the string, and by thus slightly sharpening the pitch of the note give greater prominence to the melody. It was therefore much more capable of expressing the composer's ideas than the early pianofortes and harpsichords. Forkel says that the great Sebastian Bach delighted in this instrument, as he considered it the best for study, and, in general, for private musical entertainment. He found it the most convenient for the expression of his thoughts, and he did not consider it possible to produce such a variety in the gradations of tone from any harpsichord or piano as from the clavichord, although its tone was extremely weak.

The clavicymbalum differed from the clavicytherium, the strings being disposed after the fashion of the harp. These strings were of steel instead of brass wire, and were sounded by quill plectra.

The manichord—by which name the clavichord was often called—was an instrument of great antiquity. At first the monochord, as the name implies, had but one string, which was about five feet in length, fitted up with a finger-board and bridge, and was played upon, like a double bass, with a bow; but in the eleventh century many strings had been added to it.

Although the clavichord was most probably introduced long previously in England, the first mention of it is in the year 1500, when William Cornish "composed in the Fleete" "A Treatise between Trouth and Informacion," in which the following passage occurs:—

> The clavicorde hath a tunely knyde,
> As the wyre is wrested high and low:
> The songe of himself yet neuer the les
> Is true and tunable, and sing it as it is.

After this, we find frequent mention of the instrument. Amongst the privy-purse expenses of Elizabeth of York, queen of Henry VII., the following is entered, dated August, 1502: "*Item.* The same day, Hugh Denys, for money by him delivered to a stranger that gave the queen a payre of clavycordes. In crowns for his reward iiijli."

The reward was four times greater than the estimated value of the gift, so that this royal mark of approval and appreciation of the maker's generosity, whose name unfortunately is not mentioned, is highly to the honour of the queen.

These are the earliest references to the clavichord in England, but the following extract from Caxton's translation of 'The Knyght of the Toure," which was printed in 1484, proves that it had previously to that time been in common use among the early French minstrels: "A young man cam to a feste where were many lordes, ladyes, and demoysels, and arrayed as they wold have sette them to dinner, and had on him a coote hardye after the manner of Almayne. . . . Sir Gregory called hym before hym, and demanded hym where his vyills or clavycordes were. . . . The yonge man answered, 'Syre, I can not meddle therewith.' Sayd the knight, 'I can not believe it, for ye be counterfaytted and clothed like a minstrell.'"

The clavichord-makers held in greatest repute were Wilhelme, of Cassel, and Venesky and Horn, of Dresden.

The instrument which gradually superseded the clavichord in England was the virginal. It was an improvement upon the clavicytherium, to which it was very similar, brass wire being substituted for the catgut strings. The plectrum of hard leather was replaced by a piece of raven or crow quill, attached to a small block centred in a piece of wood called the *jack*, which rose vertically from the end of the finger-key farthest from the player. When the key was pressed down, the jack moved upwards, forcing the quill past the string, which it thus set in vibration. The quill then remained above the string as long as the finger held the key down, allowing the string to vibrate freely, but directly the finger was removed from the key the quill fell on the string, and being on a centre the jack returned to its place, when a small piece of cloth fixed in the top of the jack stopped the vibrations of the string.

The touch of the virginal was extremely sensitive. It was impossible to press down a key, when the instrument was in order, without the note sounding. If, however, the key was struck a sharp blow, no greater power could be obtained than by the lightest pressure. Fétis, in speaking of the virginal and the spinet, which was similar to it except in shape, says, "When the defects inherent in the construction of the clavichord were discovered, a plan was adopted of striking the strings with small pieces of quill affixed to minute springs adjusted in the upper part of small, flat pieces of wood termed *jacks*. . . . This new invention was applied to two instruments which differed only in form. The one was the *virginal*, the other the spinet, which had the form of a harp laid in a horizontal position." The compass of these instruments was four octaves, from second added line below the bass to second added line above the treble. Their tone is well described by Dr. Burney as "a scratch with a sound at the end of it." The motion of the keys and jacks in this instrument was the cause of the well-known sarcasm of Lord Oxford, which is thus described by Isaac Reed: "When Queen Elizabeth was playing on the virginals, Lord Oxford, remarking the motion of the keys, said in a covert allusion to Raleigh's favour at court, and the execution of the Earl of Essex, 'When *jacks* start up, *heads* go down.'" The virginal was a very favourite instrument of Queen Elizabeth, and is sometimes thought to have been named after that virgin queen; but this is evidently a mistake, as her sister Mary and King Henry VIII. were both performers upon this instrument. The name *virginal* is therefore either derived, as Dr. Johnson considers, from its being principally cultivated by young ladies, or else from its being greatly used in convents, in accompanying hymns to the Virgin.

The proficiency of King Henry VIII. and his daughters as players is well attested. Queen Elizabeth must, indeed, have performed music that would be considered exceedingly difficult even now, if she really played the pieces that are in her virginal music-book, which is still preserved. Sir James Melvil, in his "Memoirs," gives an amusing account of a curious conversation which he had with Queen Elizabeth, to whom he had been sent on an embassy by Mary, Queen of Scots, in 1564. After her Majesty had asked how his queen dressed 'which of the two sovereigns dressed the better, which of the two was the fairer, and so forth, she inquired, on learning that Queen Mary sometimes recreated herself in playing upon the lute and virginal, if she played well, and was answered, ' Reasonably, for a queen.'" "The same day, after dinner, my Lord of Hunsdean drew me up to a quiet gallery that I might hear some music (but he said he durst not own it), where I might hear the queen play upon the virginals. . . . I ventured within the chamber, and stood a pretty pace, hearing her play excellently well; but she left off immediately as soon as she turned her about and saw me. She appeared to be surprised to see me, and came forward seeming to strike me with her hand, alleging that she was not used to play before men, but when she was solitary, to shun melancholy."

One of Queen Elizabeth's virginals is still in existence at Worcestershire. At the sale of Lord Spencer's effects at Chichester it was described as having a "case of cedar covered with crimson Genoa velvet, the inside of the case lined with strong yellow silk." It is light and portable, being only twenty-four pounds in weight, five feet in length, sixteen inches wide, and seven inches deep. The front is covered entirely with gold. There are fifty keys, with jacks and quills, thirty of them ebony tipped with gold, and the semitone keys (twenty in number) are inlaid with silver, ivory, and different kinds of wood, each key consisting of about 250 pieces. The paintings of the royal arms and the ornamentation give it a most beautiful appearance.

The English spinet was similar to the virginal except in its shape, which was nearly that of the harp laid horizontally, supposing the clavier or keyboard to be placed on the outside of the trunk or sounding-board. Amongst the excellent specimens of spinets in the interesting collection of old musical instruments at the South Kensington Museum is one probably made by Annibale dei Rossi, of Milan; compass, four octaves and an eighth, from E. This instrument has the inscription upon it, "Anniballis de Roxis, Medeiolanensis, MDLXXVII.," and is a most beautiful specimen, being almost covered with precious stones, as even the keys are profusely ornamented with them. An engraving of this gorgeously ornamented spinet will be found in Fig. 18, p. 97. Like the virginal, it had but one string to each note, which was set in vibration by means of the jack, with the raven or crow quill attached. When a second string was added to each note to render the instrument more powerful and capable of some slight degree of expression, it was named the harpsichord, or horizontal harp. The harpsichord was, in effect, a double spinet, as two rows of quills were used. When the performer wished to play softly, he was compelled to take one hand off the keyboard to move a stop to the right. A single string only was then twanged by the quill, the second row of jacks and quills being moved by the rail in which they were fixed so that, when raised by the key, the quills passed between the strings without setting them in vibration. If the player required greater power he would move the stop to the left again, causing the jacks to return to the proper position for snapping both the strings belonging to each note. Many rows of jacks, and in some instances an additional set of keys, were afterwards added, and other ingenious inventions were introduced into the harpsichord, until this instrument became quite an intricate piece of mechanism.

Handel's harpsichords had three or four strings to

FIG. 18.

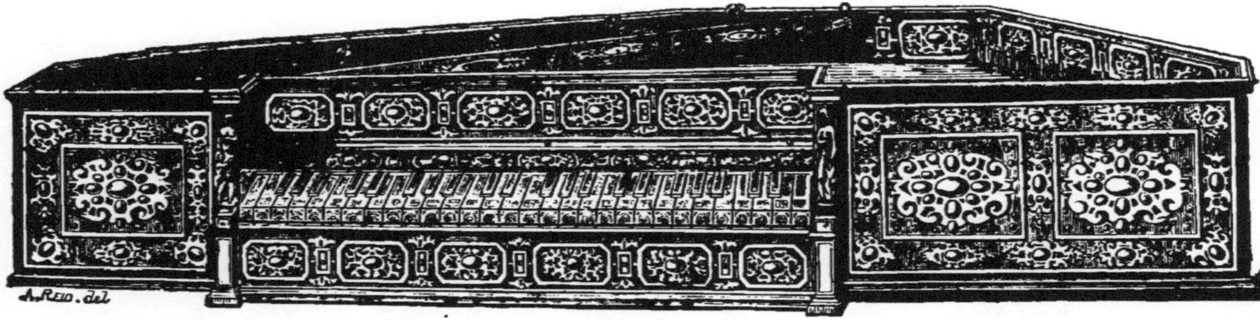

ITALIAN SPINET, ornamented with precious stones, made by Annibale die Rossi, 1577. From the "Descriptive Catalogue of the Musical Instruments in the South Kensington Museum," by Carl Engel. By kind permission of the Secretary of the Science and Art Department.

each note; one of them had four strings, two tuned in unison, the third an octave above, and a fourth tuned an octave below the two unison strings and two octaves below the highest. This was calculated to produce some effect in the great composer's music; but it was with much difficulty kept in tune. A description of the instrument bequeathed by Handel to his secretary, Smith (who wrote the music that Handel composed and dictated), will explain many of the improvements introduced in the harpsichord. This instrument (which was manufactured by the celebrated Hans Ruckers, of Antwerp, and is shown in Fig. 19, p. 101), is six feet eight inches in length, three feet in height from the ground, and three feet in width. The case is the same shape as that of the modern grand pianos, and is made of black japanned deal, with painted ornaments inside the top and upon the sounding-board. It has two rows of keys, the compass of each of which is four octaves and seven-eighths, G to F. The upper row of keys presses one quill only against one of the strings. The lower row, by use of the stops, can be made to raise quills to strike one or two strings; still further to increase the tone, a third row with finer and shorter strings under the others, with separate bridges, could be vibrated by another row of quills. By the use of the stops, the player, whilst pressing down a single key, could make two strings sound in unison, and a third an octave above, using the upper row of keys for playing the soft passages.

Handel's performance upon this instrument must have been very fine, for, even when his loss of sight compelled him to trust to his inventive powers in playing, his embellishments of the vocal and orchestral score at the Opera House, London, were so admirable that the attention of the audience was frequently diverted from the singing to the accompaniment. This marked preference often greatly mortified the singers, one of whom warned Handel that, if he ever played him such a trick again, he would jump down upon his instrument and put an end to the nuisance. Handel was excessively amused at this outburst, and, with his usual dry humour, said, "You vill jump, vill you? Very vell, sare; be so kind and tell me ven you vill jump, and I vill advertishe it in de bills." The attention of his audience was still gained by Handel, but it need scarcely be added that the threatened onslaught was not attempted. The effect of Handel's performance upon the harpsichord was not, however, due to the instrument; for such a composer and player would have made any instrument attractive. At a country church Handel played so splendidly upon a very ordinary organ that the congregation, instead of being "played out,"

FIG. 19.

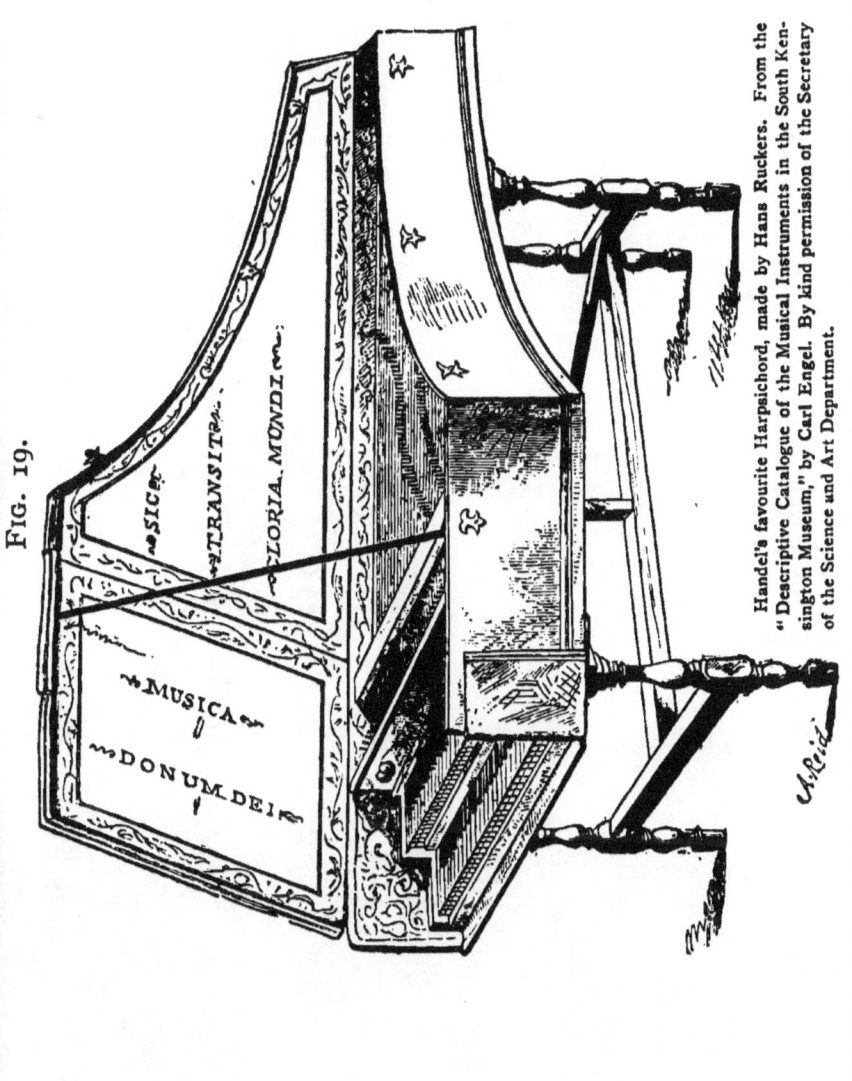

Handel's favourite Harpsichord, made by Hans Ruckers. From the "Descriptive Catalogue of the Musical Instruments in the South Kensington Museum," by Carl Engel. By kind permission of the Secretary of the Science and Art Department.

remained fixed in admiration, quite calling for the organist's impatient remark, "*You* can't play them out." He then showed Handel the way, by playing a few chords in the ordinary manner, and these speedily operated upon the people, the church being quickly cleared. Handel's favourite harpsichord-maker was Hans Ruckers, who in 1585 was the inventor of the third string tuned to the octave, and who extended the compass to nearly five octaves. Besides Ruckers and his family, the principal harpsichord-makers were Geronimo, of Florence, Coushetti and Tabel.

Merlin changed the octave stop to a third unison about the year 1770, which rendered the instrument equally powerful and less likely to get out of tune, the octave stop being affected by the least change of temperature. The quill flectra of the harpsichord so quickly wore out that various substitutes were tried, as the process of quilling took many hours; but neither leather, tortoise-shell, ivory, nor any of the substances used, were found to answer as well as the crow-quill.

It is strange to notice how old inventions, when revived, supersede improvements, or supposed improvements, that had before superseded them. Farini, a celebrated harpsichord-maker, revived a species of clavi-cytherium, which was imitated by so many German makers that the catgut-stringed instruments threatened to take the place of those with steel and brass wire, while the upright clavichord was revived in a modified shape as a new invention by Rigolo, of Florence, in 1625, under the name of the upright harpsichord. This shape was again introduced nearly two hundred years afterwards, under the name of the upright piano, as a novelty, and has almost superseded the grand in France and England.

M. Fétis, in his "Sketch of the History of the Pianoforte," refers to the numberless attempts to make the harpsichord capable of expression in playing. He says, "Harpsichords were constructed with more than twenty different modifications to imitate the sound of the harp, the lute, the mandoline, the bassoon, flageolet, oboe, violin, and other instruments. In order to produce these different effects new rows of jacks were added, which were furnished with materials of the softest kind and most conducive to expression; and yet, with all the complications of stops, springs, extra rows of keys, and Venetian swells over the strings, the grand secret—the real shading of the *piano* and *forte*—were still wanting. Nothing better was devised for augmenting or diminishing the sound than to put in motion different rows of jacks, so as to withdraw them from or approximate them to the strings at pleasure." Godfrey Silbermann, of Freiburg, made several improvements in the harpsichord about the middle of the eighteenth century, especially in the keyboard, which he extended, and in the touch, which he lightened. He also revived the clavichord in a slightly altered form, thus taking a step towards producing the pianoforte; for in this instrument, the *clavecin d'amour*, the strings were *struck* as in the old clavichord, but struck and pressed up exactly in the middle of each string by the brass wedge, which formed a middle bridge, allowing the string to vibrate in the lengths behind and in front of it. This was a step in the right direction, although a step backwards; but was not followed by any other striking mechanism for some years.

Our best English makers were the Haywards and John Hitchcock. After them, Keen, Slade, John Harris, and Rutgerus Plenius, who invented the lyrichord in 1741. This instrument, which was intended to imitate stringed bow instruments, was played upon by means of a keyboard and a treadle, that turned a circular bow used for vibrating the strings when pressed near to it by the keys' mechanism. The invention has lately been revived in a slightly modified form under the name of the *piano quatuor*.

Tabel introduced some ingenious improvements; but one of his foremen, Burckhardt Tschudi, or Schudi, acquired a still greater reputation. Another of his workmen, Jacob Kirkman, also became a celebrated manufacturer, and he was the means of restoring the harpsichord to the favour that the guitar temporarily usurped. Burney, in "Rees' Cyclopædia," article "Guitar," says that the common guitar was so much in vogue among all ranks of people as nearly to ruin the harpsichord and spinet manufacturers. Ladies sold their harpsichords for a third of their cost, till Kirkman, after spending nearly all his money in buying up these instruments for better times, made a present of a number of cheap guitars to girls in milliners' shops and ballad-singers. He then sent them through the streets singing to a few accompaniments that he had taught them. In this manner he soon made the ladies ashamed of their frivolous and vulgar taste.

The harpsichord, although so universal an instrument, was gradually supplanted by the pianoforte. As that instrument came into public favour, Moscheles, when giving his *Soirées Musicales* in 1838, had very great difficulty in finding one upon which to perform some of the lessons of Scarlatti, Handel, and Bach.

CHAPTER VII.

THE INVENTION AND PROGRESS OF THE PIANOFORTE.

The harpsichord and other instruments of the same class were extremely inefficient substitutes for the orchestra; as no improvements introduced in them could produce the same varieties of expression. It was reserved for the "orchestra of the drawing-room," the pianoforte, to accomplish this more fully.

The development of the pianoforte was particularly slow. Thousands of years elapsed before the dulcimer and harp were converted into the pianoforte by the addition of finger-keys that could raise many plectra together for the purpose of striking chords. The harpsichord-makers endeavoured to render their productions suitable for orchestral compositions, but when such players as Handel, Bach, Beethoven, Haydn, and Mozart commenced using keyboard instruments, these miserable apologies for the orchestra could not continue long in use; and when an instrument was invented by which the light and shade required for imitations of orchestral effects could be produced, it is not surprising that the pianoforte, although at first weak in tone and of short compass, should be almost universally adopted by the great composers. "The use," Thalberg says, "of this kind of instrument led to the peculiar capabilities of the pianoforte being thoroughly studied and appreciated; and the composers repaid their obligations to the instrument by writing for it many of the very finest productions of music, and by practising the execution of these productions to such an extent as to be able to bring them before the public with the greatest possible *éclat*. The importance which the instrument thus gained led from time to time to its improvement and enlargement, and this again to still finer compositions being produced for it, and to the adaptation for the pianoforte of all the best orchestral compositions; so that the advance of art and the improvement of the piano have had a mutual effect upon each other, until it is now beyond all question the first of musical instruments both to the profession and to the cultivated classes of society."

National vanity naturally causes the wish to possess the greatest number of men of genius, so that no sooner does anything really useful or novel appear, than it is claimed by half-a-dozen nations or individuals. It is not surprising, therefore, that although little more than a century and a half have elapsed since the pianoforte was invented, the name of the actual inventor is almost lost amid a crowd of claimants and appropriators. In England the invention is claimed for Father Wood, an English monk at Rome, who manufactured a pianoforte in 1711, and sold it to Samuel Crisp, Esq., the author of "Virginia," from whom it was purchased by Fulke Greville, Esq. This instrument, being the first piano seen in England, produced an immense sensation amongst musicians; for it gave skilful performers the opportunity of playing with much greater expression than was possible with any harpsichord or spinet. It was, however, defective in its action, and rapid music could not be played upon it with good effect; but when such slow pieces as the Dead March in "Saul" were performed, it was considered a marvel.

Although Father Wood's claim to the invention of the piano is often stoutly maintained, the best authenticated is that of the Italians, for in 1711 Bartolommeo Cristofali, of Padua, had already manufactured three pianos, which are thus described in the "Giornale de' Litterati d' Italia" (Venice, 1711), by the celebrated Scipione Maffei: "Signor Bartolommeo Cristofali, of Padua, harpsichord-player of the most Serene Prince of Tuscany, has already made three harpsichords, in which the production of more or less sound depends upon the force the player uses in pressing upon the keys, by regulating which not only are the *piano* and the *forte* heard, but also the degrees of tone, as in the violoncello." After speaking of the opposition this new invention met with, which he ascribes to musicians condemning it without proper trial, Maffei proceeds: "Instead of the jacks that produced sound by quills, there is a little row of hammers that strike the string from below, the tops of which are covered with leather. Every hammer has the end inserted into a circular butt, that renders it movable; these butts are partially embedded and strung together in a receiver. Near the butt, and under the stem of the hammer, there is a projecting part or support that, receiving the blow from beneath, raises the hammer and causes it to strike the string with whatever degree of force is given by the hand of the performer; hence the sound produced can be greater or less, at the pleasure of the player." The mechanism, which is then described, was ingenious, and the damping was effected by *under-dampers*—that is, the dampers acted under the strings.

From Maffei's description it seems evident that Cristofali was really the inventor of the pianoforte in 1710. He must have been a genius, for in every part of the piano, and the harpsichord also, he introduced some improvement, in the case and sounding-board as well as in the mechanism.

Although Cristofali's claim to the invention seems perfectly clear it is still disputed. Fétis, the great Belgian authority, claims for Marius, the French manufacturer, that he "submitted two instruments to the examination of the Académie des Sciences, in the month of February, 1716;" for in the "Recueil des Instruments et des Machines approuvés par l'Académie des Sciences" are found, under Nos. 172, 173, and 174, engraved plans of three instruments, termed by Marius "clavecins à maillet," with a description of the mechanism, which was very simple and imperfect, being merely a piece of wood fastened into the end of each key, which raised a hammer covered with sheepskin over the striking part. In another action, however, he approached nearer to the desired result.

That Cristofali's invention was five years at least prior to Marius's, and that it is greatly superior, is certain; but it is possible from the crudeness of the mechanism made by Marius, that he had never heard of or seen any of Cristofali's pianos, which did not gain any great success.

The claimant advanced by the Germans, Cristoph Gottlieb Schröter, deserves more than passing notice;

for, although he cannot be considered the inventor of the piano, his improvements upon Cristofali's invention were very great. Schröter, the son of an organist, was born at Hohenstein, on the borders of Bohemia, August 10, 1699, so that he was only eleven or twelve years old when Cristofali invented the piano. When eighteen years of age, and a pupil at the school of the Holy Cross, in Dresden, he constructed a model of a pianoforte, which was afterwards exhibited to the court at Dresden, and received the approval of the Elector of Saxony; but no reward was given to the inventor and maker. "In 1717," he says, "I constructed at Dresden, after much consideration, the model of a new clavier, *with hammers*, upon which one could play loudly or softly."

This invention of Schröter's was not, however, lost, for Silbermann, of Strasbourg, Spaett, of Dresden, and Stein, of Augsburg, copied it, but made Schröter no payment for using his invention without his consent. Godfrey Silbermann manufactured many pianos upon Schröter's system. After making two with great care, he submitted them to Sebastian Bach for his approval; but this was not to be obtained easily, for, after trying and examining them carefully, Bach praised the mechanism, but complained of the tone, which he said was unequal and feeble, especially in the upper octaves.

Although Silbermann was naturally chagrined at the opinion given by the great composer, this was his stepping-stone to fortune; for he was so determined to conquer the difficulty that, after many trials, he succeeded in producing an instrument which Bach declared was "without fault."

Forkel, in his "Life of Sebastian Bach," says that Frederick the Great of Prussia, who was an excellent flautist and musician, heard some of Silbermann's "forte-pianos" (so called at first to denote the newly-acquired power of playing loudly and softly). He was so greatly pleased with them that, although they were fifteen in number, he purchased the whole, placing them in different apartments of his palace. He then invited Bach, whose son, Charles Philip Emanuel, was in his service, to the palace. When at last the invitation was accepted, and Bach arrived at the lodgings of his son, the king was at one of his private concerts, but after he had seen Bach's name amongst the list of strangers, he said, "Gentlemen, old Bach is come at last." When he arrived in his travelling-dress the king took him over the palace to try the "forte-pianos" he had purchased, declaring the concert postponed. The celebrated contrapuntist then spent the whole evening with the king, who tested his musical powers most severely. He at last gave the great composer a subject on which to extemporise a fugue in six parts, but, as it was unsuitable, Bach employed a subject of his own.

Although Bach preferred the clavichord for private practice, he recommended the piano so strongly that Silbermann was wonderfully successful, establishing his reputation without a rival, and rapidly amassing a considerable fortune.

Another imitator of Schröter, John Andrew Stein, of Augsburg, whose daughter was afterwards married to Streicher, of Vienna, was a pupil of Silbermann's, and was very successful as a pianoforte-maker. Mozart, in one of his letters, dated October 17, 1777, says, "I begin, in describing different pianos, with those of Stein. Before meeting with them I thought those of Spaett were the best; now I give the preference to the first mentioned, for his are better and more commodious than the pianos of the Ratisbon manufacturer. In passages that require vigorous play I can lift the finger or leave it on the note, for the sound is not prolonged beyond the instant in which it is heard; it never shivers, nor does it ever fail to sound, as in other pianos. It is true Stein never lets a piano go under three hundred florins, but one cannot sufficiently repay the trouble and zeal he employs; his instruments have one quality found in them, and, above all, they have the escape movement, without which it is almost impossible that a piano can render a well-articulated sound. The hammers fall again as soon as they have touched the string, whether the finger be left on the key or not. When Stein has finished a piano he plays all kinds of passages upon it, and never quits it until it is capable of anything, for he labours not for pecuniary interest, but for his love of the art. He frequently says, 'Were I not myself a passionate amateur in music, my patience would long ago have failed me; but I like an instrument that assists the musician, and serves for a long time.' His pianos, in fact, are very lasting." In explaining the manner of construction, Mozart adds, " Stein warrants the solidity of his sounding-boards. When he has completed one, he exposes it to the air, rain, sun, and snow—in a word, to every atmosphere—that it may split; then, by means of slips firmly glued in, he closes the crevices. When a sounding-board has been thus prepared it may be regarded as safe against all accidents." Mozart, at some length, then praises Stein's pedals, which were pressed by the knees, and were used instead of the usual harpsichord stops, which compelled the player to raise his hands from the keyboard.

The extracts given from Mozart's letter convey an accurate idea of the perfection at which the makers and musical professors considered the pianoforte had arrived, and a general idea of the instruments themselves, which were in the shape of the square and grand, with very little power of tone and only five octaves of compass. The escape action mentioned was that invented by Schröter, whose plans had been copied by several makers.

Schröter was the organist at Nordhausen, and in 1763 protected some further inventions by patenting them. Five years afterwards he published a description of these improvements, with which, he said, "the performer can play *piano* or *forte* at pleasure." Hence he is often considered the inventor of the name *pianoforte*, if not of the instrument itself; but even this is contradicted by the record of the purchase of fifteen "fortepianos" twenty years previously by Frederick the Great, while the name itself, by which the instruments were expressly mentioned, implies that the piano was of Italian origin. Schröter was so successful a manufacturer, that he speedily realised a large fortune; but he retained his organist's place at Nordhausen until his death in 1782. In contrast to Schröter's success, it is recorded that the first pianoforte-makers, Cristofali and Marius, derived no material benefit from their inventions.

CHAPTER VIII.

PROGRESS OF THE PIANOFORTE FROM ITS INTRODUCTION INTO ENGLAND.

ALTHOUGH the pianoforte had been rising rapidly in public favour on the Continent, almost the only pianofortes in England were those made by a celebrated harpsichord manufacturer, Plenius, the inventor of the lyrichord. Having copied the crude instrument made by Father Wood in 1711, he attempted the manufacture of pianos, but with little success, as the harpsichords were generally preferred. There seemed, indeed, to be a universal desire to return to the harpsichord, to which the piano was for a long time inferior in many respects. Even King Frederick of Prussia seemed to have partly considered the harpsichord superior, for, in 1765, he ordered one of the best harpsichords that the great London maker, Burckhardt Tschudi, could produce. This is not altogether to be wondered at, as the harpsichord had for a long time been manufactured very extensively, so that numerous improvements had been introduced in it, bringing it to the greatest perfection of which it was capable; whilst the pianoforte, being a comparatively new invention, and not manufactured in such large numbers, was in its infancy. The event which seems partly to have turned the tide of public opinion in England was the arrival of twelve working pianoforte-makers in 1760, who came over in search of employment. They were familiarly known as the "twelve apostles," as they succeeded in converting the English partiality for the harpsichord into love for the pianoforte. All the pianofortes made in England were in the shape of grands, until Zumpé, a German, commenced making small square instruments in 1760. This application of the virginal form to the pianoforte is claimed by Fétis for Frederici, of Gera, an organ-builder, who made square pianos in 1758, two years before Zumpé. The tone of Zumpé's pianos was sweet, and the touch was good; and as these excellent qualities were combined with low prices, convenience of shape, and power of expression in playing, his instruments suddenly grew into such favour that Zumpé was unable to supply the demand for them in England and France. An authority of the time says that in nearly every house throughout the kingdom the older stringed instruments were replaced by these pianos. Zumpé was one of the successful pianoforte-makers, and he realised a large fortune before retiring from business. Many anecdotes are told of his cheerful glass and well-filled pipe, without which, in those days, a German did not acknowledge that he lived.

Backers, a harpsichord-maker of the second rank, had constructed several pianos before Zumpé, but his success was not great; for, although he improved the mechanism, his instruments lost the spirit of the harpsichord, and gained nothing in sweetness of tone.

In 1763 John Christian Bach, an excellent organist, pianist, and composer, one of the sons of the great Sebastian Bach, gave a series of concerts in conjunction with Abel, at which he introduced the pianoforte, playing the compositions of the best German masters upon it. This use of the instrument for public performance brought it into such favour that England was soon invaded by a fresh band of German manufacturers, and the harpsichord-makers also commenced manufacturing pianofortes. Musicians perceived the superiority of the pianoforte over the harpsichord, writing many of their best pieces expressly for it, and Haydn alone composed sixty pianoforte sonatas. The instrument upon which Gluck composed his celebrated "Armida" and other works was made by Johannes Pohlmann in 1772, and was exhibited in the International Exhibition of 1862.

Accepting it as a fair specimen of the pianos of that period, some slight description may be of interest. It is a square piano; the length is four feet and a half, and the width two feet, with a small square sounding-board at the end. The strings are little more than threads; so thin, indeed, that a moderately hard blow would break them; but as the action is very imperfect, and the hammers are merely a few thicknesses of leather glued over the heads of the horizontal levers working on hinges, these strings were sufficiently thick to bear the weak blows that were struck upon them. It is difficult to conceive how such players as Beethoven, Haydn, and Mozart could have used an instrument which seems so utterly useless and insignificant when compared with the fine pianos of the present time; but the necessity of the composer to have some imitation of orchestral effects immediately at his command was doubtless the reason for its success.

Pianofortes were not used in private only; for besides the notices of Bach's performance, there is a playbill still in existence from which the following extract is taken:—

For the benefit of Miss Brickler, 16th May, 1767.

* * A the end of the first act Miss Brickler will sing a favourite song from "Judith," accompanied by Mr. Dibdin on a *new instrument called the pianoforte.*

Some writers upon music have mentioned Mason, the favourite poet, as the inventor of the pianoforte. This is a mistake, although Mason introduced several important improvements. The writer of the article "Pianoforte," in the "Encyclopædia Britannica," published in 1810, says, "The piano has been called a national instrument, because it is said to have been of English contrivance, the invention of the celebrated poet Mason." Mention of Mason would hardly have been necessary had not several learned foreign writers upon musical instruments supposed that the English founded their claim to the invention of the piano upon Mason's improvements.

These and other improvements assisted in rendering the pianoforte very popular as a concert instrument, to judge by the announcements still extant. One of these mentions that Michael Arne would preside at the pianoforte in the orchestra during the performance of "Lionel and Clarissa" at the Dublin Theatre.

In the year 1751, John Broadwood, a young Scotch carpenter and joiner, about twenty years of age, arrived in London, and succeeded in obtaining a situation in the employ of Tschudi, where he rapidly rose into favour with Mr. and Miss Tschudi. Like the proverbially good apprentice, he married his master's daughter, and became his partner and successor.

In 1776, Becker, or Backers, assisted by John Broadwood and another workman in the employment of Tschudi—Robert Stodart—after many experiments, succeeded in producing the grand action which was used by Stodart until the time of the dissolution of the celebrated firm founded by him. This mechanism has been used by the firm of John Broadwood and Sons, with slight modifications, until the present time. The first mention of a grand pianoforte made with this action is found in the books of Tschudi and Company, under date 1781.

Another celebrated manufacturer, Sebastian Érard (or Erhadt, rather), is well worthy of notice. He was the eldest of the four children of an upholsterer in Strasbourg, and was born April 5, 1752. When eight years of age he commenced the study of architecture, perspective, linear design, and practical geometry, at the schools of his native city; and to this Erard ascribes his success. His early acquaintance with drawing and the principles of mechanics was undoubtedly of great service to him.

When only sixteen years of age, Sebastian Erard found himself the head of his family, for his father, having married when advanced in years, died whilst his children were all quite young. The lad then courageously set off for Paris, as he fancied that there he would have a greater chance of success than in Strasbourg. By his talent and perseverance he became the chief workman of a harpsichord-maker, but was at last discharged, as he was "too inquisitive, and wanted to know too much." Another maker, being unable to execute an order he had received, sought out young Erard and gave it to him, reserving the right of affixing his own name as maker. When the order was completed, the supposed maker, not being able to explain the mechanism, was compelled to refer to Erard for explanation. This fact, and Erard's other harpsichord improvements, being extensively circulated in Paris in the musical world, so greatly increased his reputation that the Duchess of Villeroi heard of him, and engaged him to execute some inventions the plans of which she had herself designed. When twenty years of age, Sebastian Erard manufactured his first piano, in imitation of the English instrument, and this so greatly increased his reputation that he received numerous orders for similar instruments, sent for his brother, Jean Batiste, and with him founded the house of Erard.

The Revolution drove him to England, where, in 1794, he patented some harp improvements. He returned to Paris two years afterwards, when affairs were quieter. In 1808 he patented his celebrated invention of the double action in the harp. He died August 3, 1831.

Another well-known maker, Ignace Pleyel, was born in the year 1757, at Rupperstahl, near Vienna. He was the *twenty-fourth* child of Martin Pleyel, a village schoolmaster, and of a lady of noble birth, who was disinherited by her parents on account of her imprudent marriage. His mother died at his birth, and his father, marrying again, had a *second family* of fourteen, and died at the age of ninety-eight. A Hungarian nobleman, Count Erloedy, perceiving the talents of Ignace Pleyel, acted as his patron, paid all expenses of his tuition under Haydn, and allowed him to visit Italy, where he was introduced to the king. As chapel-master of Strasbourg Cathedral, and composer of many excellent works, Pleyel is honourably remembered. He was, however, so persecuted by his political enemies that he was compelled to leave Strasbourg and settle in Paris in 1805, where he soon became celebrated as a pianoforte-maker. In 1834, his son Camille and Kalkbrenner, his partner, manufactured a thousand instruments in the course of the year, and employed two hundred and fifty workmen. This was considered an enormous number, although it would certainly not be thought so now.

These four, Broadwood, Stodart, Erard, and Pleyel, were at this time the principal pianoforte-makers.

In 1774 Joseph Merlin tried to effect a compromise

between the harpsichord and the piano which had nearly superseded it. He patented a compound harpsichord and piano, five octaves in compass, the two instruments being played together or separately at will. When one of the pedals was pressed by the foot, the performer played upon one row of strings only; pressed a degree lower, two were struck; pressed still lower, the octave was sounded with them. This, the inventor said, "produces the swell of the organ." Robert Stodart patented a somewhat similar instrument three years afterwards, but the pianoforte by itself was preferred to these combinations.

John Broadwood's first patent, dated July 17, 1773, states that it is "for his new-constructed pianoforte, which is *far superior to any instrument of the kind hitherto made*." It was principally for the position of the wrest-pins and the shape of the hammers and dampers.

The first action of the pianoforte, properly so called, was extremely defective when compared with that to which we are now accustomed; it was, in fact, the clavichord brass wire in the key, with a leather button on the top, as in the second figure in illustration No. 17, on p. 87. When the key was pressed down the button struck the hammer against the string, causing it to vibrate. This simple but imperfect action was generally known by the name of "the old man's head." At the extreme end of the key the sticker, or *mopstick*, as it is termed, raised the damper at the same moment that the hammer was impelled against the string. The damper was a wooden lever, lying horizontally over the strings, with a piece of cloth attached to the free end. This action continued long in use, even to the commencement of the present century. The blow it gave upon the string was very weak, so that the tone it produced greatly lacked power; and it had this serious defect that, unless the key was struck with considerable force, the hammer did not reach quite up to the wire, and consequently no sound was produced. If, to remedy this, the hammer quite reached the string, with a strong blow it would *block*—that is, the hammer would remain against the string after the blow had been struck, and thus stop its vibrations. To remedy these defects several *escapement* actions were invented, which raised the hammer so near to the string that a slight blow caused it to strike, and the hopper escaped or slipped from under the hammer, allowing it to fall away from the string, as in fig. 3, illustration No. 17, p. 87. All these actions, however, had one serious defect. After the hopper had raised the hammer and had "escaped," the hammer fell upon it or else upon the hammer-rail, and after a heavy blow rebounded to the string, damping the vibrations and injuring the tone. This was remedied by the introduction of a leather-covered *check*, which caught the head of the hammer after it had struck its blow and fallen down, where it held it until released by the removal of the finger from the key. This check-action was known in England by the name of the *grand action*, and in Germany as *die Englische Mechanik*. The great improvement of the check, however, caused a defect which required a remedy. After the hammer had fallen, it was necessary for the key to rise to its position of rest before the note could be repeated, but the upward motion of the hammer was prevented by the check. This difficulty has been found the greatest of all in pianoforte mechanism, for the hammer, while held securely, must always be ready to strike again. Many attempts were made to overcome the obstacle, but none perfectly succeeded.

In 1792 John Geib, the inventor of an action well known as the *grasshopper*, attempted to revive the clavichord in combination with the pianoforte, with separate sets of keys, but he had little success.

As the mechanism of the piano improved, the thin wire with which the instruments were strung was found to produce less tone than thicker wire. Several makers tried stringing their pianos more heavily, but they found that, although the wooden framing of the case was sufficiently strong to bear the tension of the thin wire, the strain from the thicker metal was so much greater that instruments thus strung did not stand in tune. Joseph Smith, in 1799, and Broadwood, in 1808, introduced metal bracings to assist the case in withstanding this extra pressure. When John Broadwood, the founder of the justly celebrated firm of John Broadwood and Sons, died in 1812, at the advanced age of eighty-one, he was succeeded by his son James Tschudi Broadwood. A fellow-workman of his, Robert Stodart, succeeded Americus Backers, founding the firm known so long and honourably as John William and Matthew Stodart, a firm that was almost unrivalled until a few years since, when the last partner retired and would not suffer any other house to trade upon the name. Robert Stodart patented many valuable inventions, such as his "Grand Forte-Piano, with an octave swell," which produced various fine tones at the will of the player, and is especially worthy of mention. Two of his workmen, Thom and Allen, in 1820 patented an excellent system of bracing, with hollow metal tension bars applied over the strings of the grand pianos. These metallic tubes were fixed firmly at one end, and at the other were made movable in a slide, which allowed them to expand or contract in the same degree as the strings, so that great strength was given to the instrument; and changes of temperature made little difference to the tuning of pianos constructed upon this system, which was adopted by Stodart in all his grands.

The English pianos differed widely from all others, as they were powerful in tone, and the touch was firm when 'compared with the continental instruments. Nearly all the latter were finished with the simple but flimsy "Viennese action." In 1782 John Godfrey Hildebrand constructed a piano with a novel species of action and construction. It was in the shape of a square piano, with the sounding-board covering the whole length of the instrument. The hammer struck downwards, the action being above the string; but the position being contrary to gravitation, this action has never been successful, although Streicher, Petzold, Wornum, Pape, and many other makers have attempted to perfect it. The compass of the pianoforte was only five octaves and a half until Francis Panormo, an excellent pianist and musician, suggested the advisability of extending it; but no pianoforte-makers ventured to make this alteration until John Broadwood and Sons tried the experiment. Their first addition was half an octave of keys in the treble to C altissimo, and the scale was afterwards carried down to CCC in the bass, thus extending it to six octaves. The compass was next carried up to F in the treble, forming six octaves and a half; and when another note was added, G, it was termed six octaves and three-quarters. After this, the addition of the treble A made the compass six and seven-eighths octaves, and that of the bass notes to A formed the complete seven octaves. These additions were made at different and irregular times, as the mechanical resources of manufacturers became enlarged, and the music written for the instrument extended in compass.

In the year 1800 Muzio Clementi and Frederick W. Collard commenced business. Clementi was the son of an embosser in silver at Rome, and was born there in the year 1752. He displayed great musical ability, and when nine years of age obtained an organist's situation in his native city. When twelve years old he composed a mass for four voices, which Carpani, his master, was compelled to applaud, although he added that had he been consulted "the mass might have been better." When the famous Peter Beckford was at Rome he heard the juvenile organist play with such taste and execution that he brought him to England, and undertook his musical education at his seat in Dorsetshire. At eighteen years of age "the young Roman," as Clementi was called, displayed such remarkable talent as a pianist and composer that he achieved a most brilliant success, rivalling Mozart, of whom he was a firm friend. He became connected with the firm of Longman and Lakey in 1767. The name of the firm was afterwards changed to that of Clementi, Collard, and Collard. Clementi's name, and his intimate acquaintance with Haydn, Mozart, and numberless other celebrated musicians and noble patrons, lent a prestige to the firm that quickly raised it to an equality with the oldest-established houses.

From this time the harpsichord was entirely superseded by the piano, and as the few remaining harpsichord-makers turned their attention to the improvement of pianos, these instruments attained great excellence in a surprisingly short time. One of the greatest of the improvements introduced was Sebastian Erard's repetition action for grand pianos, patented in 1821. The improvements he had previously introduced—the upward bearing of the strings and his system of constructing the grand case—were eclipsed by this invention, and the name of Erard is now always associated with his celebrated grand action. The repetition of a note in this action is perfect and the touch is light. Although extremely complicated, the mechanism is excellently constructed, and has been very generally adopted in grand pianos. Sebastian Erard patented several attempts to obtain a repetition combined with that which is as essential, a perfect check, in the *upright* pianoforte, but failed to produce a simple one, although his efforts resulted in producing an excellent check action *without* the repetition. This improvement upon Robert Wornum's action, patented in 1826, is still in use throughout the Continent and America. Especial praise is due to Wornum for his numerous inventions, the principal one of which is the "tape action."

CHAPTER IX.

INVENTION AND PROGRESS OF THE UPRIGHT PIANOFORTE.

THE square and grand pianos only have been mentioned in the preceding chapters. In both of these instruments the strings are placed in a horizontal position. In addition to these there are pianos of an *upright* form in which, with the exception of the *oblique*, the strings are vertical. The oblique and the cross-strung oblique are in the form of upright pianos, and are generally classed with them; but they are in reality totally different instruments, as the strings run obliquely from the bass end to the lower corner of the treble, and are of greater length than those in the upright, although the obliques are not usually so high as the cottage pianos. Greater power of tone and compactness of form are thus gained, but at an increased cost in the construction of the case.

The form of the grand, which is the same as that of the harpsichord, was probably suggested by the varying length of the strings. Being exactly suited to the introduction of the best mechanism, and the length of sounding-board and the strings producing a finer tone, this is the best shape for tone as well as for touch, and is always the one in which the finest instruments are made. Grand pianos are of three kinds—the concert, the semi or drawing-room, and the boudoir grands; these names denoting the length. The terms *bichord* and *trichord* imply the number of strings to each note in the tenor and treble of the instrument.

The square piano varies in shape and size, the grand square, rather a large size with grand action, being the principal. The shape of the square, like the clavichord, is oblong rectangular;—an exceedingly awkward shape in manufacture, as it renders it difficult to strengthen the framing sufficiently: the oblique position of the action and keyboard also are objectionable. These faults and its ungainly appearance have caused the use of the square to be discontinued except in India and America.

The grand and the square were the only classes of pianos manufactured until grands were set on end and raised two or three feet from the ground upon legs, and the instrument was played from the lower end.

This, the *upright grand*, was so unwieldy, from its great height, that the *cabinet*, invented by Southwell, in 1807, or by Hancock, a musical instrument maker in Westminster, a few years earlier, quickly superseded it. The cabinet was formed by the frame of the piano being brought down to the ground, and the tone was produced by the action of connecting rods and levers from the keys, which caused the hammers to strike against the strings. It formed an elegant piece of furniture, and continued long in favour, although its great height—six feet—and length of action were unfavourable to delicacy of touch. In 1811 Robert Wornum reduced the height to between four and five feet, under the name of the *harmonic*, a name afterwards changed to *cottage* piano. Sixteen years later its height was still further reduced by him to three feet and a half, under the name of the *piccolo*. The cottage and piccolo pianos became very popular, and have almost superseded the grand for private practice in England and France. The cost of these instruments was much less than that of the grands, although such exorbitant prices were paid for them to the principal firms that they were beyond the reach of the middle classes. However, a great change commenced in 1835, when John Brinsmead, founder of the firm of John Brinsmead and Sons, began manufacturing really excellent pianos at moderate prices, and several other good makers followed his example. The result was that, when these instruments had been thoroughly tested by some years' use, the idea that an instrument could not be made properly for less than eighty guineas was abandoned, and good pianos at moderate prices had a large and increasing sale.

Many inventions patented at this time have since been revived as new discoveries. John Schweiso patented a wrest-plank of cast iron instead of wood, which has since been reintroduced. John Godwin in 1836 obtained a patent for his arrangement of the strings, part of them running obliquely over the others. This also has been lately revived in America and upon the Continent with great success. Charles Wheatstone in the same year patented an invention for making a note sustain as long as the finger kept the key pressed down. This was accomplished by means of apertures slightly larger than the diameter of the string, through which a current of air passed, keeping the string in vibration. James Stewart, who was in the employment of Collard and Collard (and previously a member of the firm of Chickering in America), patented many excellent improvements in the mechanism of the piano.

An invention patented by Alexander Bain in 1847 was one in which several instruments could be performed upon simultaneously by the intervention of an electro-magnetic apparatus. The pianist played upon a piano, the keys of which worked temporary magnets in connection with the other instruments to be used, so that the act of one player could be transferred to several similar or even dissimilar instruments. This invention was most ingenious and well worthy of success; but other inventions for which patents were granted were as ridiculous as Bain's was ingenious. Daniel Hewitt, for instance, lost twelve thousand pounds in a few years through attempting to introduce a down-striking grand piano, known as the "camel-back" from its peculiarly ungainly appearance. In a patent dated December 16, 1854, he proposed affixing a wrest-plank and bent side (the two parts that together carry the strings) to the brick or stone wall of an apartment, so as to avoid the necessity for constructing costly framework, with strong bracing to resist the tension of the strings, between which and the wall he placed his sounding-board.

John Dewrance in 1855 patented a system of cast-iron framing instead of wood, and his invention is now much imitated in America.

The Exhibition of 1851 had a most beneficial effect upon pianoforte manufacture; for comparison of the instruments of different individuals and nations must necessarily have a good result. The conclusions arrived at from this comparison were that England had far outstripped every other nation in the manufacture of pianos.

The Council Medal was awarded to Erard, of London. at the Exhibition of 1851. Fétis, the deputy-chairman of the jurors in 1862, noticed this; and in his report paid a deserved compliment to the English makers, especially mentioning John Broadwood and Sons, Collard and Collard, Hopkinson, Kirkman, and John Brinsmead and Sons, each of which firms had patented great improvements in the grand and upright instruments. Of John Brinsmead and Sons he said, "Their productions have fixed the attention of the jury by their excellent construction, the perfection of their mechanism, and the most satisfactory quality of their tone."

Griener and Sandilands exhibited an ingenious but complicated appliance for tuning the three strings to each note in a piano at the same time, and another invention of a set of organ pedals to be used with the piano. Each pedal pulled the wide end of a wedge-shaped plectrum between two thick strings behind the performer, producing a pedal-pipe quality of sound. There were also several inventions of Montal exhibited, to which additional interest was attached from the fact that the inventor is blind. These, like many other inventions exhibited, were far more ingenious than useful, although they were worthy of great commendation. A clever arrangement of the loud pedal action prevented the confused sound generally arising from its unskilful use, by allowing only the first notes struck to remain sounding whilst all others were stopped by the dampers. This arrangement has lately been introduced in America. The bridge of reverberation or duplex scale for producing sustained effects, invented by Collard and Collard, also has been improved and introduced in the United States.

The American pianos were well represented by Steinway and Chickering at the International Exhibitions of 1862 and 1867, but the tone produced from them, although very powerful, was hollow, and not of a sweet, sustaining character.

The result of this competition was so decidedly in favour of the English pianos that continental makers commenced imitating them, and England was for a time inundated with common low-priced foreign copies. But these proved to wear so badly, that they quickly lost the favour their low prices and showy appearance had gained.

At the next great International Exhibition, that of 1867, the English manufacturers were as successful as they had previously been, for they were awarded the highest gold medal; and, to quote from the Report of the Jurors, "After Broadwood and Sons come Kirkman and Son and John Brinsmead and Sons in the manufacture of English grand pianos. John Brinsmead's firm is younger in this industry, but he constructs his instruments with great care. He has invented a new system of mechanism which is very ingenious, and by which the rapid repetition of the note is perfected."

This firm introduced such important improvements in their pianofortes, that in 1870 they obtained the "Grand Gold Medal of Honour" at Paris; at Amsterdam they gained the Diploma for Extraordinary Merit; at the London and Paris International Exhibitions they were awarded First Class Prize Medals, and at the latter city they received the highest distinction, the Grand Diploma of Honour, for the rapid advance they had made. In 1876 they received the Grand Prize Medal and Diploma of Honour of the Philadelphia Centennial Exhibition, and in 1877 they were awarded the Gold Medal of Honour and Diploma of Merit at the South African Exhibition.

The number of makers exhibiting pianos of ordinary manufacture naturally suggests the oft-repeated question, "Where do all the pianos go?" In the "London Directory" alone we find the names of more than 200 pianoforte manufacturers. If each of these makers produce ten per week, there are at least 104,000 pianos manufactured annually *in London alone*. When it is remembered that there are large factories in France

Austria, Germany, and throughout the continents of Europe and America, it is no wonder that the question still arises, "Where do all the pianos go?" "*To pieces*," is the answer respecting the mass of rubbishingly cheap pianos. As to the well-made instruments the inevitable effects of time and climate influence even the most solid and durable mechanism. The wear and tear from use and abuse, especially of those instruments employed in teaching, are probably some of the causes. Augmented population, and increasing love and cultivation of music amongst all classes, are also serious items. One of the principal causes, however, of such numbers of pianos being made is the rapidly progressive improvement of the mechanism used in their construction, which constantly induces, almost compels, the affluent classes to reject the pianos they possess, not because time and use have impaired them, but because the genius and invention of makers have placed before them instruments with better touch and more powerful tone. The old instruments are sold and resold until pianos that have graced mansions are found in the humblest cottages.

The Netherlands International Exhibition of 1869 contained some excellent pianos, those of Herz and John Brinsmead and Sons having been especially noticed. The advance in manufacture made by these firms is an illustration of the improvements introduced, which compel those who can afford the outlay to purchase an instrument from which such superior quality and volume of tone are produced with perfect ease and certainty. The improvements patented by John Brinsmead, in 1862, 1868, 1871, 1875, and 1879, throughout Europe and America, result from the most simple means, and this very simplicity insures the durability of the piano. The mechanism in these instruments, both in the upright and in the grand, produces every effect for which the Erard action has been so long and justly celebrated, in the most simple manner. Besides a clear, uninterrupted, and sustained tone, as well as a perfect check and repetition, it secures an extremely light yet firm touch, and one that seems to sympathise with the player, so rapidly and unfailingly does it express his ideas.

The superiority of the English pianofortes over all rivals is due partly to the solidity of their construction, which produces the lasting qualities for which they are so celebrated, and partly to the simplicity and excellence of the mechanism, the importance of which cannot be over-estimated. I may have unintentionally omitted to mention many excellent manufacturers of pianos in Great Britain. For instance, the firms of Cadby, Ralph Allison and Sons, Challen and Son,

B. Squire and Son, H. Ward, George Russell, and William Eavestaff are worthy of special praise, as they manufacture good pianos at moderate prices. At the Paris International Exhibition of 1878 the Cross of the Legion of Honour was conferred on the head of the firm of John Brinsmead and Sons; and gold medals were awarded to Erard; Pleyel Wolff and Co.; Herz; Schroeder; Hopkinson; Ehrbar; etc. Pianos now seem almost to have reached perfection. What will the next great invention be? Perhaps the sustaining power will be obtained without the aid of such devices as a current of air to keep the string in vibration, the resined barrels and bows in imitation of the violin, or of the second hammer that produces the disagreeable *tremolo* by its repeated blows; indeed, Mustel, of Paris, has already introduced a small piano in which tuning-forks are *struck* instead of strings, and this gives greatly increased vibration of tone.

CHAPTER X.

USEFUL HINTS UPON SELECTING, AND PRACTICAL DIRECTIONS FOR TUNING PIANOS, AND REPAIRING SMALL DEFECTS.

IN the selection of a piano even good judges are sometimes deceived, few being able to decide correctly until after the instrument has been in use for some months. The piano may sound well in the room in which it stands, and yet sound badly in a carpeted and furnished apartment. Care should therefore be taken to select a piano with a *sustaining* quality of tone—that is, that a note struck in any part, except the extreme treble, should continue sounding for some time after it has been struck, and the key has been held down. This is the best test of an instrument, for a piano with a sweet, sustaining quality of tone will sound well in any room.

The only means of being certain that a piano is well made of seasoned materials is by purchasing one manufactured by a good maker, whose reputation would suffer were his name placed upon an inferior instrument. Some makers rely on the name made by the founders of their houses, instead of the quality of their manufacture; and preference should be given to those who are rapidly rising to fame by the recommendation of the instruments they produce. Not only are their pianos lower in price, but they are also generally better than those manufactured by firms which, trusting to their repute alone, are slowly but surely losing it. On the other hand, the so-called "cheap pianos" must be avoided; for a really good pianoforte cannot be made at a very low price, as either the materials or workmanship must be inferior.

The sales by auction, and by "the widow of a musician," or any of the various means employed for disposing of cheap, trashy pianos, are now too well understood to be trusted.

The instrument, having been selected, must be taken care of. As it is extremely susceptible to damp and change of temperature, it should never be placed against an outer wall, or too near the fire, door, or open window. Damp being one of the greatest destroyers of the piano, a short distance from the fire and from the inner wall is the best position. It must be kept free from dust, pins, and beads, as these often cause a jar or a note to stick down. The polish should be carefully rubbed up every morning with a soft duster. The keys also should occasionally be cleaned. A damp duster can be used for this purpose, and the whole should afterwards be polished up with a dry piece of linen or silk. In damp situations the steel strings should be carefully wiped every day with a dry duster. A thick woollen cover or blanket should also pass over the instrument during the night. wherever there is much moisture in the atmosphere. The top should not be loaded with music-books and ornaments, as they absorb the tone, and the ornaments often cause a jarring sound. The instrument should be tuned five or six times in the year, especially when new, as otherwise the pitch gradually falls and the tone suffers.

It is impossible to explain tuning fully, as much must necessarily be learned by experience. A few useful hints only will therefore be given, such as will enable an amateur with a musical ear to alter any notes that may get out of tune, and to put on and pull up a new string should one break. An excellent scale will also be added for those who may already be able to tune.

The intervals of greatest importance in tuning are the *octave*, the *fifth*, and the *fourth*. The *unison* is also very important, as fully half the strings are tuned by it.

After seating himself at the piano, with a tuning-fork and hammer, the tuner may strike any note, the two strings of which will sound like one if they are perfectly in tune. Then, placing the hammer upon one of the wrest-pins, round which one of the strings is wound, the hammer may be turned a very little to the left, and the note when struck will now sound greatly out of tune. After striking it several times slowly, and listening attentively to the sound, the hammer must be turned slowly and imperceptibly to the right, the tuner paying great attention to the vibrations of the strings, until the quick beats or undulations cease, and one steady and apparently single sound, which constitutes the real unison, is produced.

When the *unison* has been mastered by patient practice the octaves may be attempted. These, when perfectly in tune and struck together, like the unison, appear to produce but one sound. The action must be shifted by pressing the left pedal with the foot, unless a tuning-wedge is used for damping the second string, so that only one string of each note is struck. The same plan as that for learning the unison tuning may be adopted for the octave, but care must be taken that the unison of the note is tuned afterwards.

The intervals of the fifth and fourth are not so easily distinguished as those mentioned. When perfectly in tune, a steady complex sound is heard.

In tuning or *laying* the scale or bearings, great practice and many verbal lessons are necessary, so that it is only requisite to give the best scale now used, and the trials, without entering into details which would be of little use.

As the pianoforte is an imperfect instrument—having no *real* B sharp and E sharp—these two intervals have to be made up by each key being equally and slightly out of tune. Hence the necessity of *tempering* the fourths and fifths, which has given the new scale the name of *equal temperament*. One rule, when properly understood and practised, will enable the tuner to produce a good and equal scale. That rule is—tune all the fifths towards the bass a wave sharp and all the fourths a wave flat.

In this scale, which is intended to explain the order and manner in which the intervals are to be tuned and the trials made, the position of the curved lines denotes whether the intervals are to be sharp or flat. Where the curves are placed *under the slur*, the fourths or fifths must be a *wave flat;* but when they are *above*, those intervals are to be tuned *sharp*. The waves are plainly perceptible in the scale we have given, but in tuning they must be almost imperceptible except to the tuner. The trial-chord, when struck, should produce a rapid *beat* or series of undulations of sound; those with the close intervals—the first, fourth, sixth, and eighth chords—sounding rather more roughly in tune than those with the more widely spread intervals.

USEFUL HINTS UPON SELECTING PIANOS, ETC. 149

It will be seen, upon reference to the scale, that after pitch C has been tuned in unison with the tuning-fork, the octave below must be "tuned perfect," that is,

without a wave. The G below is then to be tuned from C, a *trifle flat*. The D above must now be taken from G a *shade flat*, and A from D also *slightly flat*. F must then be tuned from C, a shade sharp, and the first trial, F, A, C, can be made. B♭ must be tuned from F a wave sharp, when the trial-chord is F, B♭, D. E from A, B from E, F♯ from B, and C♯ from F♯, should then *all* be tuned *slightly flat*, each interval being proved by the trials marked in the scale. E♭ when tuned from B♭ and A♭ from E♭ must both be a shade *sharp*. The trial C♯ to G♯ will then prove if the *front* and *back scales* are properly tuned, as G♯ should be slightly flat to C♯.

The gradations of sharp and flat intervals have been mentioned as though well defined, but this is not the

L

case in tuning, as they should be perceptible to the practised ear of a tuner alone.

In tuning it is very important to *set the pin* properly. The hand should be removed from the hammer before a note is considered perfectly in tune, as it sometimes requires so trifling an alteration that the mere pressure or tap of the hand upon the hammer to the right or left will supply it. When the pins are turned about much, the instrument will never *stand* in tune. After each string has been tuned, a heavy blow upon it should be given to ascertain if it hangs upon the bridge pins, in which case it would quickly get out of tune. The hammer must not be pressed up or down on the pin in tuning, as pianos are often injured by the pins being bent and broken off in this manner.

In putting on a new string, all friction that will heat the wire must be avoided, and the wire must be of the same thickness exactly as the broken string that it replaces. To insure its standing in tune, the string, when on the piano, may be stretched by pressing downwards the point where the hammer strikes with a piece of hard wood covered with leather, and tuned until the pressure upon the string does not cause the pitch to fall.

As a knowledge of how to properly repair small defects in the piano may be of use, the principal of these and their remedies shall now be described.

The *sticking of keys* is generally caused by damp, which swells the wood, making the mortices too small for the pins to work in. To remedy this the key must be taken out, and the tight mortice carefully filed at the part where the black marks show the pin has rubbed, care being taken that the mortice is not made large enough to cause a rattle.

Squeaking of the hoppers, when the key is pressed down, is remedied by blackleading the tops of them, or burnishing them with a smooth piece of steel.

The *rattling of keys* may be cured by exchanging the key-pins for larger ones, or inserting a small wedge on one or each side of the loose mortice.

Defects in the damping are generally caused by the dampers not covering the strings properly, and requiring shifting to their proper positions.

The *sticking of the hopper* is generally caused by the top of it being rough, or by its spring being too strong. In the first case, burnish it with a piece of steel; in the second, weaken the spring by drawing it out from the top.

The sticking of a hammer is sometimes caused by its catching the damper wire or head, but it is frequently from the centre wire on which it acts becoming too tight from damp.

T *blocking* of a hammer against the string may be

altered by turning the button in the hopper until the hammer falls when pressed up near the string.

Jarring, so common in pianos, is generally caused by some small piece of wood or metal touching the string or sounding-board, or else by the vibrations of the strings between the lower bridge, and the hitch-pins being insufficiently damped, by the list drawn between them. Loose frets or ornaments about the piano will also produce these disagreeable sympathies.

Hammers touching the wrong string may be altered by heating the hammer-shanks with a hot iron, and pressing the hammer in the direction required.

When the *wrest-pin jumps* in turning, it should be replaced by a freshly resined one, or else either chalk or powdered resin should be put upon it and in the hole, before it is again inserted in the plank.

To *deepen the touch*, brown paper or a thin card should be placed under the *balance-rail*—the middle rail under the keys—near the screws, which must be taken out to allow the paper to be forced under. To make the touch *shallower*, a card or single thickness of brown paper should be placed under the *front* rail.

APPENDICES.

INVENTIONS PATENTED BETWEEN THE YEARS 1693 AND 1879 A.D.

Oct. 20, 1694.—GEORGE JOYCE and P. EAST. Self-acting harpsichord, etc.

Oct. 22, 1730.—JOHN HARRIS. Harpsichord (no description).

Dec. 17, 1730.—WILLIAM BARTON. Metal plectra in spinets, etc.

Dec. 30, 1741.—ROGER PLENIUS. Ivory and tortoise-shell plectra.

July 10, 1745.—ROGER PLENIUS. Harp stop and bushed keys.

Dec. 18, 1769.—BURKAT SHUDI. Venetian swell over the strings.

Dec. 28, 1770.—THOMAS HAXBY. "A single harpsichord of two unisons ... which produces ten variations of stops."

May 2, 1771.—RICHARD WAKEFIELD. Ivory and metal plectra, and wrest-pins.

Aug. 29, 1772.—ADAM WALKER. The "Celestina," in which the catgut strings are vibrated by circulating bands of silk, etc.

Sept. 12, 1774.— JOSEPH MERLIN. "A set of hammers, of the nature of those used in the kind of harpsichord called pianoforte, are introduced [in a perfect harpsichord] in such a manner that either may be played separately, or both together. . . . By placing the foot upon [the pedal] it gradually plays one unison, one degree lower plays the second unison, and lastly the octave, which produces the swell of an organ."

Dec. 28, 1774.—S. GILLESPY. Harpsichord with "a peddle and swell," by which the top of the instrument is raised and the stops worked.

Nov. 21, 1777.—ROBERT STODART. Combined harpsichord and piano.

July 17, 1783.—JOHN BROADWOOD. Position of wrest-pins and dampers, also making the "sounding-post, that communicates the sound to a sounding-board, of the same thickness and quality as that on which the bridge is fixed."

March 11, 1786.—G. J. CHEESE. "Grand Harmonica," with the strings stretched by weights, and struck by hammers. Strips of glass ranged in a frame produce sounds also, by means of balls set on wires, or by coming in contact with wheels rapidly revolved by a treadle.

Nov. 9, 1786.—JOHN GEIB. (1) Buff stop for pianos and harpsichords, screwed under the strings, and (2) "grasshopper action."

Jan. 15, 1787.—W. THOMPSON. System of tuning by means of a monochord with movable bridges.

March 31, 1787.—JOHN LANDRETH. (1) Centring the jack in square piano with cork. (2) The same, or "some woolly substance manufactured after the manner of a hat," is introduced in the upright pianoforte.

May 25, 1787.—HUMPHREY WALTON. (1) Pedal for causing the grand hammer to strike one, two, or three strings; the hammers "striking perpendicular hammers which strike the wires. . . . (2) The touch is regulated according to the fancy of the player, from the deepest to the most delicate [by] a regulating touch frame," inserted between the balance rail and the back rail of the key-frame.

Jan. 15, 1781.—SAMUEL BURY. "The instrument is a perfect pianoforte," which, by means of whalebone plectra fixed in a sliding-board, and a slide which throws up the dampers, produces sounds "exactly similar to the dulcimer and harpsichord.

Aug. 15, 1788.—C. CLAGGET. (1.) Piano called Teliochordon. "Besides the ordinary ones, two other bridges are placed nearer to the hammers, but in a just proportion, according to the musical division of the string." Metal bars press down the strings by means of pedals, causing the original bridges to lose their power, thereby producing a more acute sound as the string is shortened by the secondary bridges and metal bars. (2) The keys are covered with glass or enamel, in place of ivory. (3) Another instrument has tuning-forks or single rods of metal, instead of string, set in vibration by means of finger-keys and action.

April 13, 1790.—JOHN HANCOCK. (1.) Small pieces of leather between the strings, to deaden one string to each note, when required by the player. (2.) A back sticker "presses down a palate at the bottom of pipes," in a case below the pianoforte, admitting wind from a bellows blown by a pedal. This flute-stop can be used separately or in conjunction with the pianoforte.

Nov. 16, 1790.—JAMES BALL. Square piano action, with under-dampers, and a screw in each key, for making the touch deeper or more shallow. "The hammers are fixed by means of screws that press" on the centre wire.

Feb. 4, 1792.—G. GARCKA. Position of wrest-pins and sounding-board.

April 18, 1792.—JOHN GEIB. Combination of clavichord or spinet with pianoforte, "with two sets of keys to which either of these three instruments may be joined and played together."

June 6, 1792.—JAMES DAVIS. Combined piano and harpsichord. "The upper row of keys is for the pianoforte, and the lower for the harpsichord."

Oct. 17, 1794.—SEBASTIAN ERARD. Two methods for escapement of the hammer, and an arrangement for striking one, two, or three strings at pleasure, by a side movement of the damper rail, etc. Harmonic octave produced by mechanism which pressed on the string exactly in the centre.

October 18, 1794.—WILLIAM SOUTHWELL. Improved dampers, and addition of treble keys.

Jan. 12, 1795.—WILLIAM STODART. "An upright piano in the form of a bookcase," in which "both the hammers and dampers are returned by weight."

Jan. 31, 1797.—WILLIAM ROLFE and SAMUEL DAVIS. Vellum, parchment, pasteboard, etc., varnished or oiled for sounding-boards, instead of wood.

Nov. 8, 1798.—WILLIAM SOUTHWELL. New method of applying additional notes. The frame turns down over the keys, and the "leader" is fastened to the hammer by a joint of leather. A harp played with keys is also mentioned in the specification.

Oct. 3, 1799.—JOSEPH SMITH. Introduction of metal

bracings in place of wood, " so as to admit the introduction, into the internal part of the instrument, of a drum, tabor, or tambourine, with sticks or beaters," as well as a triangle; all being brought into action by levers and cranks.

July 31, 1800.—PETER LITHERLAND. "A method of keeping [pianos, etc.] in tune by means of" helical and other springs.

Nov. 13, 1800.—ISAAC HAWKINS. Spiral springs in place of long bass strings. The strings are fixed in a perpendicular position, ranging from three to four feet in height to within a few inches of the floor. By means of " primary and secondary carriages, . . . two, three, or more strings may be stretched at the same time" in tuning, "and they may be put in tune one with another, by turning the screws of the secondary carriages." A roller with pins acting upon levers shortens any strings, at the pleasure of the player, by pressing on and dividing them into varying lengths. The " poiatorise " stop is produced by another roller, which, revolving rapidly, causes projections upon it to strike on the hammers, thus keeping them continually striking the strings whilst the keys are held down. Between the hammers and the strings pieces of leather, of varying thickness, are introduced, so as to change the tone gradually from *forte* to *piano*. The key-frame is made to turn on pivots, for economy of space. Besides these improvements a *volti subito* is introduced, which, by the use of the pedal, turns over the leaves of the music-book when required.

May 16, 1801.—SEBASTIAN ERARD. "The touch rendered either hard or soft to any degree, at the election of the player."

June 5, 1801.—EGERTON SMITH and THOMAS TODD. Tuning by means of screw and lever, or by a wheel, axle, and pulley; which allow of "any number of strings being drawn up by one weight over a wheel or axle."

Nov. 7, 1801.—JOHN CONRAD BECKER. Half and quarter tones, produced by causing the wrest-pins to move partly round their centres, thereby altering the tension of the string as may be required.

Nov. 10, 1801.—A. BEMETZREIDER, and RT. J. and A. SCOTT. "Horizontal harp" piano; the top opens at the back, forming a swell.

Nov. 28, 1801.—EDWARD RYLEY. Movable keyboard for transposing music simply by shifting the keyboard and action.

March 9, 1802.—THOMAS LOUD. Upright pianos rendered portable by placing the strings *in an oblique direction,* "fixing the first bass strings from the left-hand upper corner to near the right-hand lower corner, and the rest of the strings in a parallel direction. By this means an instrument standing only five feet high and four feet wide in front will admit of the bass strings being their full length, which is five feet two inches."

March 24, 1802.—PETER LITHERLAND. "Helical, spiral, or straight springs, for keeping the strings to their tension" and the piano in tune.

June 28, 1803.—GEORGE WOODS. Strings attached to pulleys, beams, etc., so that the whole may be raised or lowered in pitch at once.

Jan. 23, 1805.—ED. THUNDER. "Screw rest-pin."

April 8, 1807.—WILLIAM SOUTHWELL. Cabinet pianoforte and action.

July 25, 1808.—WILLIAM HAWKES. "Two sets of strings of two unisons to each set." The action being shifted by a pedal so as to strike each set, produces " seven diatonic and five flat tones to our present scale of twelve fixed tones."

Sept. 24, 1808.—SEBASTIAN ERARD. Repetition action, which "affords the power of giving repeated strokes, without missing or failure, by very small angular motions of the key itself.

July 26, 1809.—DAVID LOESCHMAN. "By means of six pedals that cause the hammers to act upon twenty-four distinct sets of strings," performers can "play in thirty-three perfect keys."

May 2, 1810.—SEBASTIAN ERARD. The tuning-pins inserted in a collar and socket for ease and smoothness in motion.

March 4, 1811.—WILLIAM SOUTHWELL. Piano *sloping backwards*, with improved action and damper wire.

March 4, 1811.—J. TROTTER. New keyboard arrangement.

March 26, 1811.—ROBERT WORNUM. "Improved upright pianoforte," with diagonal strings. Buff-stop for stopping one string of each note is worked by a pedal.

April 24, 1811.—WILLIAM BUNDY. Bass pianoforte strings covered with platina or other metal to produce powerful sounds by vibration.

Sept. 9, 1811.—WILLIAM FREDERICK COLLARD. Square pianoforte "turned upwards on its end."

March 3, 1813.—FREDERICK HAUCK. Method of applying "additional keys, strings hammers, etc. . . . to old-keyed instruments."

Dec. 9, 1813.—JOHN BATEMAN. "The Grand Clavilyr." "The strings may be struck at or near the middle . . . in a similar manner to that of the finger upon the strings of a harp, by playing upon keys."

May 14, 1816.—WILLIAM SIMMONS. Barrel piano or harpsichord.

Oct. 14, 1816.—JOSEPH KIRKMAN. Two strings in unison and one with separate bridges tuned to the octave above, are struck by one hammer, forming an "octave stop."

Nov. 14, 1816.—JOHN DAY. Frame of musical glasses played separately, or in combination with the piano, by finger-keys and action.

Feb. 1, 1817.—ISAAC MOTT. "The Sostinente pianoforte" produces a sustaining tone through the strings being vibrated by a revolving roller, by means of silken lines attached to them. A movable bridge presses against the centre of the strings, and produces the harmonic octave effect by dividing them into two equal lengths.

Jan. 15, 1820.—JAMES THOM and WILLIAM ALLEN. Metallic tubular bracing to counteract the tendency of pianofortes to get out of tune from the swelling and contracting of the wood caused by atmospheric changes.

May 13, 1820.—ROBERT WORNUM. One size wire used for stringing tenor and treble. The length of the first note is determined on the monochord, "and for all the corresponding notes upwards you must halve the several notes, and so on for as many octaves as you require, always halving for the last octave." This is intended to produce equal tension throughout the instrument.

March 8, 1821.—WILLIAM FREDERICK COLLARD. "The bridge of reverberation" is a third bridge below the two others to allow that part of the strings which is generally listed, or damped, to sympathise and vibrate in unison with the lengths between the ordinary bridges.

April 5, 1821.—WILLIAM SOUTHWELL. Check action applied to cabinet pianos, to prevent the hammer "rebounding against the strings."

Dec. 22, 1821.—PIERRE ERARD. (Communicated.) Repetition check action for the grand pianoforte.

Jan. 14, 1821.—D. LOESCHMAN and J. ALLRIGHT. In the "patent Terpodion" sounds are produced by friction on wood, metal or any hard substance, played with pianoforte keyboard.

Feb. 18, 1823.—FRANCIS DEAKIN. Improvement in steel wire and mode of fastening it.

July 24, 1823.—HENRY SMART. Check acting on the hammer.

Nov. 22, 1823.—THOMAS TODD. The strings are vibrated by a roller upon each side of the strings, when brought in contact by the key and action.

July 29, 1824.—WILLIAM WHEATSTONE. External surface covered with frames having vellum, etc., tightly drawn across, with trumpet-mouthed holes, for augmenting the tone of the pianoforte.

Jan. 5, 1825.—PIERRE ERARD. Wrest-plank and

key-bottom united by pieces of sheet iron placed between the two sides of the case. New application of patent of 1821.

Jan. 18, 1825.—FRANCIS MELVILLE. Metallic bracing for square pianos.

Feb. 6, 1825.—G. A. KOLLMAN. Down-striking grand-action and larger sounding-board.

Oct. 6, 1825.—JAMES SHUDI BROADWOOD. Check action applied to square pianos.

July 4, 1826.—ROBERT WORNUM. (1) Hopper and two check actions. (2) "Pizzicato pedal."

Feb. 20, 1827.—PIERRE ERARD. Application of action to square pianos, 1821 patent.

March 22, 1827.—JAMES STEWART. Wire put on without loops or "eyes," by making one continuous string pass round a single hitch-pin, so as to produce the effect of two separate strings.

April 9, 1827.—JAMES SHUDI BROADWOOD. Metal string plate in the grand piano.

July 25, 1827.—EDWARD DODD. Both bridges upon sounding-board. The quality of tone is regulated by a brass nut and screw at the back of the hammer-head.

Aug. 30, 1827.—W. DETTMER. Screws for altering the pitch.

July 10, 1828.—J. H. A. GUNTHER. A second thicker sounding-board, with the belly-bridge upon it, is placed over the ordinary one.

July 24, 1828.—R. WORNUM. Check acting on the back part of the lever.

Aug. 11, 1829.—THOMAS ROLFE. Improved self-acting pianoforte.

Nov. 2, 1829.—J. STEWART. Brass rail applied to back part of action frame.

Feb. 27, 1830.—SIMON THOMPSON. Upright pianoforte, having the top level with the lockboard.

Feb. 2, 1831.—J. C. SCHWIESO. Cast-iron wrest-plank.

July 20, 1831.—W. ALLEN. Cast-iron grooved frame with the wooden wrest-plank driven tightly into the grooves.

Sept. 8, 1832.—F. P. FISCHER. Down-striking grand action.

Nov. 1, 1833.—JACOB ZEITTER. Sounding-board bars made of two or more pieces.

Jan. 15, 1835.—J. STEWART. Escapement action.

Sept. 1, 1833.—F. DAVCHELL. Hammer shanks, suspended by an india-rubber thread to the butt. Hollow bridge on sounding-board.

Nov. 6, 1835.—R. WOLF. "Shell of curvilinear shape, in lieu of the usual sounding-board."

May 13, 1835.—P. FISCHER. Cross-strung piano. "In order to increase the length, I place the strings diagonally, and they then pass under the other strings."

Feb. 17, 1836.—J. LIDEL. (1) Sounding-board free, being fastened at one end only. (2) *Piano* effects are produced by the stroke of the hammer being shortened.

March 8, 1836.—J. GODWIN. Strings run over others, or are placed across them, in square pianofortes.

May 14, 1836.—WHEATLEY KIRK. Double sounding-board and complete metallic framing or support.

July 27, 1836.—CHARLES WHEATSTONE. Continuous sounds produced from pianoforte strings or springs, by means of currents of air which pass through apertures slightly wider than the body the air vibrates.

Aug 24, 1837.—W. SOUTHWELL. Spring applied to hammer butt, to obtain repetition.

Feb. 21, 1839.—JOHANN STUMPFF. Improvements in mechanism and tuning apparatus.

July 2, 1839.—H. PAPE. Sounding-board reversed and placed behind the bracings in a console-shaped piano.

Feb. 14, 1840.—J. CLARKE. Free sounding-board, one part only being firmly fixed.

Sept. 24, 1840.—PIERRE ERARD. Improvements in mechanism and string plate.

Nov. 7, 1840.—E. DODD. Set of strings on the back, as well as a set in front, of the frame, acting as a counterbalance, and "double pianoforte."

June 23, 1841.—J. GODWIN. The wrest-pin block is placed *above* the strings in the grand.

July 7, 1841.—J. STEWARD. Complete metal framing to carry the strings. Upright pianoforte action, proceeding downwards, strikes near the under bridge.

Nov. 11, 1841.—J. STEWART. Escapement action.

Jan. 15, 1842.—T. LAMBERT. Improved cabinet action.

Feb. 2, 1842.—HENRY BROADWOOD. Name-board with pictorial representation "of the extension of the black and white keys for learners."

Feb. 15, 1842.—R. WORNUM. The "tape check action."

Feb. 11, 1843.—H. DU BOCHET. Repeating square action.

Jan. 19, 1843.—J. G. KIRKMAN. Improved action (no specification).

April 29, 1843.—J. STEWART and T. LAMBERT. Cabinet repetition action.

June 26, 1844.—CHARLES SAUTTER. Continuous sounds produced by a succession of shocks from hammers put in vibration by a revolving cylinder.

Oct. 10, 1844.—OBED COLEMAN. Æolian attachment. Reeds are attached to the bottom of the pianoforte-case, and are acted upon by wind. They are played separately or in combination with the pianoforte.

Nov. 9, 1844.—DANIEL HEWITT. Striking simultaneously in different parts of the string, etc.

Dec. 12, 1844.—S. MERCIER. "Transposing piano."

April 7, 1845.—W. HATTERSLEY. Metallic elastic trusses for strengthening the framing.

Oct. 27, 1845.—B. NICKELS. Two actions and sounding-boards, and two sets of strings and keys, are employed for producing a combined upright and horizontal pianoforte.

Nov. 11, 1845.—S. CROMWELL. Elastic stops for producing harmonic sounds when pressed upon the strings in the centre of them.

April 28, 1846.—ISAAC MOTT. "Metallic skeleton," applied to stringed instruments, to resist the pressure caused by the tension of the strings.

June 16, 1846.—F. BURKINYOUNG. Down-striking grand action.

July 8, 1846.—T. WOOLLEY. Movable key-bed and frame.

April 29, 1847.—J. SPEAR. India-rubber applied between the movable parts to prevent noise.

Oct. 7, 1847.—ALEXANDER BAIN. Electricity employed for playing several instruments simultaneously.

Aug. 12, 1850.—C. CADBY. Sounding-board strained like a drum.

Sept. 12, 1850.—PIERRE ERARD. Metallic wrest-plank.

Dec. 20, 1850.—J. PAPE. Vibrations of the strings increased by air, etc.

June 3, 1851.—J. HOPKINSON. "Clothing the hammers with sponge." Action with sticker jointed in the middle.

Nov. 15, 1851.—PIERRE ERARD. "Laying the wires on or against the sounding-board."

Nov. 20, 1851.—T. STATHAM. Metallic stop to the wrest-plank and sounding-board, for the purpose of relieving the latter from the pressure of the strings.

Jan. 27, 1852.—T. LAMBERT. Bevelled lever.

Jan. 31, 1852.—WILLIAM SQUIRE. Gravitation employed in a new check-action, instead of springs.

July 15, 1852.—H. GAUNTLETT. Pianofortes and organs played by means of electricity.

Oct. 1, 1852.—G. BROCKBANK. Two wrest-planks, between which the strings pass.

Oct. 1, 1852.—J. STEWART. Stop for the hammer at the back of the lever.

Nov. 17, 1852.—H. RUSSELL. Flattened wire, in place of round pianoforte strings.

March 7, 1853.—W. MATTHEWS. "Propeller action," to prevent "blocking" in damp situations.

March 17, 1853.—J. ASHENHURST. Hollow wood bracings and bridges.

May 30, 1853.—H. HUGHES and W. DENHAM. Continuous sounds, produced by two sets of hammers being successively brought into action.

July 6, 1853.—R. Rüst. Sound-holes in the sounding-board, with metal tubes passing through hollow bars inserted.

Aug. 16, 1853.—J. Stewart. Connecting the sticker with the fore end of the lever, the back end being hinged to the lever-rail in the upright pianoforte.

Oct. 6, 1853.—Joseph Cary. Single check action with "loop and spring."

Dec. 22, 1853.—J. Shaw. Construction and arrangement of the action and bracings.

May 1, 1854.—W. Waddington. The ribs or bars in front, instead of at the back, of the sounding-board.

May 8, 1854.—G. Thomas. Bracings dovetailed into the body of the wrest-plank.

May 25, 1854.—J. Harrison. Metallic wrest-plank and improved lever.

Aug. 23, 1854.—W. S. Smith. Rounded bridges with plates of metal.

Oct. 12, 1854.—F. Delsarte. Apparatus for tuning.

Nov. 3, 1854.—E. Alexandre. Combination of organ and piano.

Dec. 16, 1854.—D. Hewitt. Piano constructed against any strong wall: the wall supplying the place of "costly framework with strong bracings."

Dec. 19, 1854.—William Dreaper. Application of compensating-bars and generators of sound to the sounding-board and bars.

Jan. 22, 1855.—J. PAPE. Tuning-fork piano.

April 28, 1855.—JAMES MARSH. Piano capable of being separated for portability.

May 2, 1855.—T. LAMBERT. Hopper-head connected with the hopper by a regulating screw.

Oct. 13, 1855.—JOHN DEWRANCE. Cast-iron framing, with wrest-plank secured in a metal-frame by bolts, and covered with a plate of soft metal.

Nov. 1, 1855.—S. DRIGGS (U.S.). Metallic framing, with sounding-board within an independent metallic frame, which holds it in an arched form.

Nov. 23, 1855.—J. FISHER. Reversible hammer-head.

Jan. 3, 1856.—F. GUICHÉNÉ. — Connecting-rods, which cause chords of the note to sound when a single key is struck.

Jan. 25, 1856.—W. OWEN. Second sounding-board.

Feb. 13, 1856.—W. MOUTRIE. Springs acting upon the dampers.

Feb. 26, 1856.—J. STEEDMAN. Arched bars "for the support of the sounding-board and central bridge."

April 16, 1856.—F. PRIESTLY. "Rocking lever or butt to each key, . . . constructed with a hammer-shank and hammer."

July 11, 1856.—A. N. WORNUM. Repetition grand action.

Oct. 9, 1856.—J. and E. SHAW. Separate strings for *sharps* and *flats*.

Oct. 10, 1856.—D. SHIRLEY (U.S.). Simplified action, "to render it cheap, . . . and to prevent blocking."

Nov. 6, 1856.—J. LA CABRA. Arrangement of sticker and check.

Dec. 1, 1856.—J. C. HADDON. Metal framing, "and loading the bass strings with buttons, . . . placed upon them so as to obtain deep notes" with short lengths of strings. The strings are galvanised or tinned, "to preserve them from oxidation."

Feb. 26, 1857.—WILLIAM MILLS. Escapement upon the upper part of the sticker.

April 9, 1857.—T. ROLFE. Vulcanised or plain india-rubber, in place of wire, for a "check."

May 11, 1857.—S. HALLETT. Strings are arranged "concentric with the sound-boards. One, two, four, six, or eight keys" may be applied to the same instrument.

May 13, 1857.—H. TOLKIEN and J. MIDDLETON. "Hard wedge or wedges," inserted in the bracings for strength.

May 14, 1857.—G. CRAWFORD. Upper bridge entirely of glass. The sounding-board has a double bridge, indented with bone or ivory instead of pins.

July 25, 1857.—F. OETZMANN and T. L. PLUMB. Hopper acting directly on the hammer-butt.

Sept. 3, 1857.—T. JACKSON. Check upon hammer-butt by sticker.

Oct. 30, 1857.—M. STODART. Reduction in thickness of sounding-board, from the bridge outwards, towards each edge where it is fixed.

Nov. 11, 1857.—H. and S. THOMPSON. Additional stickers, for producing an octave or chord at will, when a single key is struck.

May 13, 1858.—A. WOLFF. "Independent pedallier."

Sept. 21, 1858.—JOHN DEWRANCE. Compensating bars in bass of piano.

Oct. 2, 1858.—J. and E. HOLMAN. Upright pianoforte action.

Nov. 17, 1858.—J. ROBERTSON. Thicker sounding-board, with the surface grooved out "longitudinally in parallel lines."

Dec. 9, 1858.—R. BURROWES. Set of rectangular cranks, to elicit the sound of two notes by the touch of one key.

Dec. 9, 1858.—J. STEWART. Hopper escapement action.

Feb. 11, 1859.—C. JACKSON. Escapement hopper.

Feb. 11, 1859.—C. MILLS. Improved hopper.

Aug. 15, 1859.—C. GLASSBOROW. Sounding-board

and strings in front, and a second set behind the bracings, to produce equal tension and sympathetic vibration of the two sets of strings.

Aug. 30, 1859.—JAMES HARE.—Improvement in wrest-pins and string-plate.

Sept. 6, 1859.—J. STEWART. Improved escapement action.

Oct. 4, 1859.—G. GREINER. (1) Appliance for tuning two strings at the same time. (2) Pedallier with leather covered plectra for pulling the strings.

Nov. 30, 1859.—F. MATHUSEK (New York). Sounding-board, strings, etc., are arranged so as to make them somewhat similar in action to instruments of the violin class.

Jan. 2, 1860.—DR. HÜRLIMANN (Zurich). Light "wooden frame. ... Metal bars, ... placed between the sounding-board and the strings, ... extend in the same direction, ... and are fastened to the wrest-plank near the piano-pins, and below on the iron plate on which the strings are fixed."

April 17, 1860.—S. B. DRIGGS (U.S.). Graduated sounding-board and bridge.

April 28, 1860.—T. MOLINEUX. Single check action with loop and spring.

May 21, 1860.—C. DE MEYER. Two sounding-boards "fitted on metallic construction of framework."

APPENDIX A.

May 29, 1860.—W. NOSWORTHY. Sounding-board passing under detached metal bridge.

July 28, 1860.—J. PAPE. The hammers "have two, three, and even four faces, instead of a single one," to replace the surface worn by use. The height of this piano is two and a half feet only.

Aug. 3, 1860.—C. WILLIAMS and E. F. FALCONER, (U.S.). Bells instead of strings.

Aug. 27, 1860.—J. P. PIRSSON (U.S.). The "Trylodeon," a combination of the piano and harmonium.

Sept. 25, 1860.—CARL KIND. Repetition grand action.

Dec. 29, 1860.—H. VINER. "One set of keys transmits motion to two sets of hammers, . . . one to strike up [on the strings in the grand piano], and the other to strike down" upon a second set of strings tuned in unison with, or an octave above or below, the upper set.

Feb. 2, 1861.—W. PRANGLEY. "Rise [in the key] at a point before it reaches its centre-pin."

May 21, 1861.—WILLIAM DREAPER. "Tie-rod is applied to . . . the bars of the sound-board in such manner as to draw such bar or bars into a bent form."

June 20, 1861.—J. L. CLEMENT. To overcome the non-continuity of sound, "an arrangement somewhat similar to the bow of a violin," acting separately, or simultaneously with the hammers, is added to the piano.

July 11, 1861.—J. R. COTTER. Strings pulled by claw-shaped plectra in the middle of their length.

July 18, 1861.—B. JOHNSON and W. H. ANDERSON. Double sounding-board, with "swell valves" and "the *very forte* pedal" for sounding octaves.

Nov. 16, 1861.—R. T. WORTON. "Lyro-pianoforte." A pianoforte and harpsichord combined.

Dec. 3, 1861.—R. A. RÜST. Sloping front and sliding extended desk.

Feb. 11, 1862.—JOHN BRINSMEAD. Grand and upright mechanism for producing "a perfect check, great power, . . . and quick repetition."

Feb. 13, 1862.—WILLIAM WILLIAMS. Diagonal bass strings, inclining towards the right in grand pianos, and continued below the keyboard towards the front of the keys.

Feb. 26, 1862.—C. L. KNOLL. Connecting-rods from the keyboard to cause the action to strike upon strings at the back of the instrument.

Feb. 26, 1862.—E. G. BRUZAUD. Two dampers for each note.

March 10, 1862.—W. S. NOSWORTHY. Keyboard, pedals, and seat raised above the usual height, enabling vocalists to read the performer's music.

March 20, 1862.—J. G. THOMPSON. Enharmonic scale and shifting keyboard.

April 7, 1862.—THOMAS JACKSON. Spring on end of sticker that causes a check.

April 14, 1862.—J. M. FRENCH. Hollow wooden bracings.

April 19, 1862.—A. N. WORNUM. Improved damper.

April 30, 1862.—H. F. BROADWOOD. Metal plate over the wrest-planks of grands, tapped to receive wrest-pins upon which either a male or female screw has been cut.

May 9, 1862.—G. F. GREENER and I. H. C. SANDILANDS. Improved grand action.

May 22, 1862.—G. CRAWFORD. Small pianoforte with metal prongs instead of strings.

June 23, 1862.—R. COOK. Metal employed for tops of hoppers.

June 28, 1862.—G. H. HULSKAMP. Compressed sounding-board.

Aug. 27, 1862.—J. J. POTTER. Improved upright action.

Sept. 11, 1862.—J. MOLINEUX. Sticker action with check.

Feb. 5, 1863.—R. A. BROOMAN (FRANÇOIS DELSARTE). Method of tuning two strings simultaneously.

Feb. 13, 1863.—S. M. INNES. Transposing keyboard.

March 16, 1863.—W. G. EAVESTAFF. Check action.

April 29, 1863.—W. FARR and E. FARR. Improved action.

July 31, 1863.—B. JOHNSON. Combination of piano and organ.

Sept. 30, 1863.—W. CLARKE. Combined piano and organ or harmonium.

Nov. 12, 1863.—G. H. BROCKBANK. Perforated metal plate between sounding-board and strings.

Nov. 20, 1863.—A. H. FERRY. Hammer-head made so that the coverings can be tightened or loosened.

Jan. 18, 1864.—W. H. MARKS. Piano with four strings to each note, two of which are tuned an octave higher or lower than the other two.

April 12, 1864.—R. A. KEMP. Tuning the pianoforte scale by means of twelve harmonium reeds.

April 20, 1864.—A. V. NEWTON. Action for producing increased power in short horizontal grands.

June 1, 1864.—A. V. NEWTON [JOHN WINTER JONES]. Combination of piano and drum.

June 15, 1864.—R. A. BROOMAN. Improved tuning apparatus.

July 4, 1864.—J. W. JONES. Down-striking action.

July 19, 1864.—E. LEA. Combined piano and harmonium.

Aug. 4, 1864.—T. J. V. ROZ. Transposing keyboard.

Nov. 1, 1864.—W. MOODY. New tuning apparatus.

APPENDIX A.

Jan. 17, 1865.—F. H. LAKIN. Tuning by means of levers on metal plate over wrest-plank.

March 9, 1865.—W. T. HAMILTON. Guide for the position of the hands in playing.

April 4, 1865.—W. MOODY and W. J. HULAND. New method of stringing.

June 15, 1865.—G. E. WAY. Improved metal plate in cross-strung square pianos, with repetition action.

June 26, 1865.—W. E. NEWTON. Metal frame over thin boards in sweep-side and wrest-plank.

June 30, 1865.—R. A. BROOMAN. New tuning apparatus.

Aug. 5, 1865.—H. C. BAUDIT. Violin-piano.

Oct. 5, 1865.—B. JOHNSON. Combined piano and organ.

Oct. 10, 1865.—G. G. RICH. Improved damper action.

Nov. 29, 1865.—E. FARR and J. GREGORY. Improved action.

Dec. 7, 1865.—W. E. EVANS. Transposing keyboard.

March 22, 1866.—J. MACINTOSH. Trumpet-shaped covering to be placed over the piano or vocalist, so that the tone may be augmented by means of compressed air.

April 3, 1866.—G. HASTLETINE. Pianoforte with four strings to each note, two of which are struck by an action above the keys and two by an action below the keyboard.

April 5, 1866.—B. JOHNSON. Combined piano and harmonium.

April 24, 1866.—S. THOMPSON. Octave couplers to pianoforte keys.

July 10, 1866.—J. MILLWARD. Combination of piano, couch, closet, and bureau with toilet articles. The music-stool is constructed to contain a workbox, a looking-glass, a writing-desk or table, and a set of drawers.

Aug. 24, 1866.—W. E. NEWTON [GEORGE BYRON KIRKHAM]. Movable transposing keyboard.

Sept. 4, 1866.—E. FARR and J. GREGORY. Each string passes from its wrest-pin completely round both sides of the sounding-board, so as to obtain an equal upward and downward pressure.

Nov. 28, 1866.—G. HASTLETINE [LEVI SMITH TOWER]. Improvements in the mode of, and means for, regulating and registering the tension of pianoforte strings.

Dec. 3, 1866.—M. A. F. MENNONS [JUAN AMANN]. Apparatus for performing by means of electro-magnetism.

Dec. 14, 1866.—H. BRINSMEAD. Simple check action.

Feb. 4, 1867.—J. F. PHILLIPE. Metal frame cast in one piece.

March 6, 1867.—W. E. GEDGE. Transposing action.

March 18, 1867.—H. SIMMS. Tone resonator.

May 9, 1867.—A. HERCE. Keyboard to enable performer to face auditors.

June 3, 1867.—E. MCLEAN. Arched resonator at top of piano.

Oct. 16, 1867.—W. H. MAY. Impregnating sounding-boards with salt water.

Oct. 19, 1867.—M. J. MATTHEWS. Double pianoforte strung at back and in front.

Nov. 1, 1867.—J. GILMOUR. Improved back.

Nov. 6, 1867.—A. M. CLARK. Vibrating hammer set in motion by a cylinder for producing sustained tones by continuous blows.

Nov. 16, 1867.—R. W. PEARCE. Hollow case made on violin principle and placed under feet of piano.

Feb. 27, 1868.—F. WIRTH. Assistant for raising parts only of the dampers, by means of the loud pedal.

March 6, 1868.—J. BRINSMEAD. (Perfect check repeater action) for producing perfection of touch with increased durability.

Aug. 20, 1868.—G. CALKER. Diagram of music in front of keyboard for beginners.

Sept. 1, 1868.—E. JOBSON. Hammers covered with velvet or other piled fabric instead of felt.

Sept. 16, 1868.—G. R. SAMSON. New method of stringing.

Oct. 28, 1868.—W. DAWES. (1) A zinc compensating frame. (2) Double sounding-board. (3) Mechanism for producing sustained tones by repeated blows. (4) Octave coupler.

Nov. 6, 1868.—T. HARRISON. Improved action.

Nov. 23, 1868.—C. MONTAGUE. Framing covered with caoutchouc.

Dec. 17, 1868.—J. T. HALL. Improved hinges for piano tops.

Dec. 28, 1868.—J. P. MILLS. Drawn steel wrest-pins.

Jan. 20, 1869.—T. STEINWAY. Metallic action frame.

Feb. 11, 1869.—P. J. SMITH. Metal bars under sounding-board.

April 14, 1869.—E. DOWLING. Application of T-headed screw to fly-rest.

April 28, 1869.—F. BAUER. Combined wood and metal framing.

April 30, 1869.—L. B. FORTIN.—Improvements in felt machinery.

May 26, 1869.—C. F. CHEW. Transposing double keyboard and metal bars in wooden bracings.

July 2, 1869.—J. STEWARD. Sounding-board with concave bars.

July 14, 1869.—C. BREWER. India-rubber tubes for under-covering of bass hammers.

Sept. 7, 1869.—T. KING. Check action.

Nov. 11, 1869.—J. JULES. Combined piano and organ.

April 8, 1870.—J. H. KIRKMAN. Steel bar in wrest-plank.

Nov. 23, 1870.—W. G. EAVESTAFF. Check action.

Nov. 29, 1870.—T. LAMBERT. India-rubber springs for action.

Dec. 1, 1870.—H. L. GLEIG. Sounding-board extended under metal wrest-plank "bridge."

Dec. 1, 1870.—A. N. WORNUM. Position of wrest-pins.

Jan. 8, 1871.—W. TONGUE. Flattened steel wire, kept in vibration by currents of air.

Feb. 16, 1871.—T. LAMBERT. Improved action, with zinc, lead, or tin slates on top of hoppers.

March 5, 1871.—J. BRINSMEAD. Improvements in piano action.

March 30, 1871.—F. and R. HUND. Cast-iron frame.

April 25, 1871.—A. ZEWADSKI. Octave coupler.

April 27, 1871.—D. ROGERS, J. MONINGTON, J. WESTON. Combined wood and metal bracings.

June 1, 1871.—C. F. CHEW. (1) Conical pins. (2) Adjustable tension straps. (3) Straps for strengthening bridges. (4) Hollow resonator.

June 21, 1871.—I. LIEBICH and W. PATERSON. Harp effects caused by tongues of metal placed between strings and hammers.

July 20, 1871.—W. R. NORMINTON. Self-escapement hopper.

Aug. 12, 1871.—R. GAUNT. Metal hinges.

Sept. 20, 1871.—E. MOLYNEUX. Electro-magnetic mechanical arrangement.

Oct. 3, 1871.—T. JACKSON. Improved hopper.

Nov. 22, 1871.—J. AMANN. Mechanical arrangement for playing keyboard instruments

March 20, 1872.—R. SMITH. Laminated sounding-board.

April 16, 1872.—C. S. VENABLES. Two damper pedals.

May 1, 1872.—C. A. DE LAZKAWSKI, H. KITUMAN. Tuning forks used in lieu of strings

May 3, 1872.—L. GÜNTHER. String rail.

May 14, 1872.—C. T. STEINWAY. Improved agraffe or stud.

Aug. 16, 1872.—C. F. GOFFRÉE and J. H. SCHUEL. Improved method of balancing keys.

Oct. 14, 1872.—E. B. GOWLAND.—Double bearing on bridge, with down-pressure bar.

Jan. 2, 1873.—A. D. B. WOLFF. Transposing keyboard attachment.

March 17, 1873.—J. BURTON. Metal frets.

May 6, 1873.—W. FRIUDENTHEIL. Cast-iron wrestplank.

May 31, 1873.—D. G. STAIGHT and S. STAIGHT. Alabaster or gypsum substitute for ivory.

June 18, 1873.—C. J. COXHEAD. Improved damper.

July 31, 1873.—U. C. HILL. Cellulated bell, or tuning-fork piano.

Oct. 15, 1873.—C. H. L. PLASS. Repetition action.

Dec. 1, 1873.—H. HANKINSON. Transposing keyboard.

Feb. 9, 1874.—H. CHATWIN. Mother-of-pearl in lieu of ivory.

Feb. 27, 1874.—J. H. DUNKLEY. Sounding-board carried up to top-bridge.

May 6, 1874.—J. B. HAMILTON. Coiled, flat, or round wires.

May 20, 1874.—E. ILIFF and J. RINTOUL. Simple action.

June 12, 1874.—C. J. COXHEAD. *Prolonge* on key.

July 14, 1874.—F. H. WHITEMAN. India-rubber used instead of felt in every part of the action.

July 27, 1874.—D. IMTROF. Automatic piano.

Sept. 2, 1874.—M. W. HANCTIEL. Dampers mechanically held after the strings have been struck.

Oct. 20, 1874.—W. MEAD. Combined piano and musical-box.

Nov. 23, 1874.—A. STEINWAY. Dampers mechanically held after the strings have been struck.

Nov. 25, 1874.—J. B. HAMILTON, G. WADE, and R. W. VOSEY. Compensating springs attached to strings to prevent changes of pitch.

Jan. 2, 1875.—W. R. MILLER. Insulators.

Jan. 27, 1875.—G. H. BROCKBANK. Simple action.

Feb. 19, 1875.—E. T. BURLING. A system of tuning.

Feb. 20, 1875.—G. and A. ROBERTS. Escapement action.

March 1, 1875.—J. ELLIS. Transposing keyboard.

March 6, 1875.—J. BRINSMEAD. Perfect check repeater action for producing increased durability as well as perfection of touch.

March 16, 1875.—R. H. ROGERS. Simple action.

May 13, 1875.—A. D. B. WOLFF. Stops for regulating dampers.

May 31, 1875.—T. B. HOWELL. Method of strengthening back.

July 17, 1875.—E. G. BURLING. Banjo attachment.

Aug. 21, 1875.—A. MONTGOMERY. Improved arrangement of keyboard.

Aug. 31, 1875.—W. R. NORMINTON. Transposing keyboard.

Nov. 5, 1875.—C. J. WARD. Harmonic seraphlute, with concertina keyboard applied to a stringed instrument.

Nov. 12, 1875.—A. D. B. WOLFF. Improvements in wrest-plank and pins.

April 19, 1876.—C. E. ROGERS (U.S.A.). (1) New damper. (2) Universal joint connecting key and jack. (3) Improved escapement. (4) Three springs to counteract atmospheric influence. (5) String plate and new method of tuning the strings.

May 30, 1876.—F. WIRTH. (1) Additional strings and bridges for producing the overtones. (2) Improved dampers.

Aug. 1, 1876.—G. T. BOUSFIELD. Hand-rest for position of the player's hands.

Sept. 23, 1876.—G. A. CASSAGNES. Nickel-plating of strings and metal work.

Oct. 14, 1876.—J. C. WARD. (1) The strings, hammers, and stickers are alternately placed on the opposite sides of the frame. (2) Harmonic angelute.

Nov. 7, 1876.—J. ROBINSON. Combined piano and harmonium.

Feb. 6, 1877.—J. T. WRIGHT. Combined piano and harmonium or organ.

Feb. 20, 1877.—E. LECOMTE. (1) Strings set in vibration by the longitudinal friction of prepared felt rubber. (2) The forked damper.

Feb. 27, 1877.—H. BROOKS. Improved action.

March 23, 1877.—E ZACHARIAE. Cellular boxes within the instrument to augment the tone.

Oct. 20, 1877.—J. MONINGTON and J. WESTON. Transposing keyboard.

Nov. 20, 1877.—C. PIEPER. Second row of strings and hammers for producing the octave and fundamental tones simultaneously.

Dec. 29, 1877.—H. WITTON. Improved action.

July 5, 1878.—T. HOWELLS. Portable pianoforte. The strings are stretched horizontally along the exterior of a hollow cylinder or framework; the action operates upon the strings from the interior of the cylinder.

July 23, 1878.—E. C. CADOT. Automatic equaliser for pianoforte keys.

August 20, 1878.—S. F. WASLEY. Resonators under the castors.

March 20, 1879.—BRINSMEAD, J. (1) Sostenente sounding-board, glued on rim of soft wood. (2) New form of metal plates and supports. (3) Improved repeater check action. (4) Improved sticker action. (5) Various appliances of tone-sustaining pedal. (6) Strength of sounding-board regulated by springs.

APPENDIX B.*

DESCRIPTION OF DOVE'S SIRENE, FIGS. 4 & 5, PAGE 13.

"I WILL take the instrument asunder, so that you may see its various parts. A brass tube t, Fig. 4, leads into a round box C, closed at the top by a brass plate $a\,b$. This plate is perforated with four series of holes, placed along four concentric circles. The innermost series contains eight, the next ten, the next twelve, and the outermost sixteen orifices. When we blow into the tube t, the air escapes through the orifices, and the problem now before us is to convert these continuous currents into discontinuous puffs. This is accomplished by means of a brass disc $d\,e$, also perforated with eight, ten, twelve, and sixteen holes, at the same distances from the centre and with the same intervals between them as those in the top of the box C. Through the centre of the disc passes a steel

---

* From "On Sound," by John Tyndall, D.C.L., LL.D., F.R.S.

axis, the two ends of which are smoothly bevelled off to points at p and p'. My object now is to cause this perforated disc to rotate over the perforated top $a\,b$ of the box c. You will understand how this is done by observing how the instrument is put together.

"In the centre of $a\,b$, Fig. 4, is a depression x sunk in steel, smoothly polished and intended to receive the end p' of the axis. I place the end p' in this depression, and, holding the axis upright, bring down upon its upper end p a steel cap, finely polished within, which holds the axis at the top, the pressure both at top and bottom being so gentle, and the polish of the touching surfaces so perfect, that the disc can rotate with an exceedingly small amount of friction. At c, Fig. 5, is the cap which fits on to the upper end of the axis $p\,p'$. In this figure the disc $d\,e$ is shown covering the top of the cylinder c. You may neglect for the present the wheelwork of the figure. Turning the disc $d\,e$ slowly round, its perforations may be caused to coincide or not coincide with those of the cylinder underneath. As the disc turns its orifices come alternately over the perforations of the cylinder, and over the spaces between the perforations. Hence it is plain that if air were urged into c, and if the disc could be caused to rotate at the same time, we should accomplish our object and carve into puffs the streams of air. In this beautiful instrument the disc is caused to rotate by the very air currents which it renders intermittent. This is done by the simple device of causing the perforations to pass *obliquely* through the top of the cylinder c, and also obliquely, but oppositely inclined, through the rotating disc de. The air is thus caused to issue from c, not vertically, but in side currents, which impinge against the disc and drive it round. In this way, by its passage through the sirene, the air is moulded into sonorous waves.

"Another moment will make you acquainted with the recording portion of the instrument. At the upper part of the steel axis pp', Fig. 5, is a screw s, working into a pair of toothed wheels (seen when the back of the instrument is turned towards you). As the disc and its axis turn, these wheels rotate. Finally, by the pins m, n, o, p, any series of orifices in the top of the cylinder c can be opened or closed at pleasure. By pressing m, one series is opened; by pressing n, another. By pressing two keys, two series of orifices are opened; by pressing three keys, three series; and by pressing all the keys, puffs are caused to issue from the four series simultaneously. The perfect instrument is now before you, and your knowledge of it is complete.

"This instrument received the name of sirene from its inventor, Cagniard de la Tour. The one now before you is the sirene as greatly improved by Dove. The pasteboard sirene, whose performance you have already heard, was devised by Seebeck, who gave the instrument various interesting forms, and executed with it many important experiments. Let us now make the sirene sing. By pressing the key m, the outer series of apertures in the cylinder c is opened, and by working the bellows, the air is caused to impinge against the disc. It begins to rotate, and you hear a succession of puffs which follow each other so slowly that they may be counted. But as the motion augments, the puffs succeed each other with increasing rapidity, and at length you hear a deep musical note. As the velocity of rotation increases the note rises in pitch: it is now very clear and full, and as the air is urged more vigorously, it becomes so shrill as to be painful. Here we have a further illustration of the dependence of pitch on rapidity of vibration. I touch the side of the disc and lower its speed; the pitch falls instantly. Continuing the pressure the tone continues to sink, ending in the discontinuous puffs with which it began.

"Were the blast sufficiently powerful and the sirene sufficiently free from friction, it might be urged to higher and higher notes, until finally its sound would become inaudible to human ears. This, however, would not prove the absence of vibratory motion in the air;

but would rather show that our auditory apparatus is incompetent to take up and translate into sound vibrations whose rapidity exceeds a certain limit. The ear, as we shall immediately learn, is in this respect similar to the eye."

APPENDIX C.*

"THE motion of a sound-wave must not be confounded with the motion of the particles which transmit the wave. In the passage of a single wave each particle over which it passes makes only a small excursion to and fro, the semi-length of which is called the *amplitude* of the vibration, the time occupied during one vibration being called its *period*.

"4. The intensity of a sound is proportional to the square of the maximum velocity of the vibrating particles. It also approximately varies inversely as the square of the distance from the origin of the sound; for supposing the latter to be produced at a uniform loudness, the same amount of energy has to be communicated to the particles contained within the external and internal surfaces of shells of the same thickness but of different *radii*. For example, if we take a shell of air whose internal radius is one foot, one of the same thickness whose radius is two feet will contain four times the quantity of

---

* From "A Dictionary of Musical Terms" (article, "Acoustics"), by Dr. Stainer and W. A. Barrett, Mus. B.

matter; one whose radius is three feet, nine times the quantity, and so on. Thus the amount of matter over which a given quantity of energy has to be distributed augments as the square of the distance from the origin of sound, and therefore the amount of energy or, what comes to the same thing, the intensity of the sound diminishes in the same ratio.

"5. At a temperature of *zero Centigrade* sound is propagated at the rate of about 1,090 feet per second, and this speed augments about two feet per second for every additional degree of temperature; thus at 15° C. the rate of propagation would be about 1,120 feet per second. The velocity of sound in air depends on the elasticity of the air in relation to its density. It is also directly proportional to the square root of the elasticity, and inversely proportional to the square root of the density. Now for a constant temperature the elasticity varies as the density; hence in this case they neutralise one another, and the velocity of the sound is independent of the density of the air.

"6. One sound differs from another not only in quantity but also in quality and pitch.* The pitch of a sound depends on the number of vibrations per second by which it is caused: the greater this number is the higher is the sound, and *vice versâ;* thus pitch is a more or less

---

* For the cause of the different qualities of sound see § 16, p. 197.

relative term, and it is therefore necessary to have some standard to which different sounds may be referred. This standard is so chosen that the middle C of the pianoforte shall be produced by 264 vibrations per second.*

"10. As the character of a sound depends upon that of the vibrations by which it is caused, it is important to know of what kind the latter must be in order that they may give the sensation of a perfectly simple tone, *i.e.*, one which the ear cannot resolve into any others. Such a vibration is perhaps best realised by comparison with that of the pendulum of a clock when it is swinging only a little to and fro. Under these circumstances it is performing what are called harmonic vibrations, and when the air particles in the neighbourhood of the ear are caused by any means to vibrate according to the same law as that which the pendulum follows, and also with sufficient rapidity, a perfectly simple tone is the result. Such a tone is, however, rarely heard except when produced by means specially contrived for the purpose. If a note on the pianoforte is struck, the impact of the hammer on the string throws it into a state of vibration which, though periodic, is not really harmonic; consequently we do not hear perfectly a simple tone, but one which is in reality a mixture of

---

* That is, according to German pitch; at present there is no definitely fixed standard in general use in England.

several higher simple tones with that one which corresponds to the actual length of the string. The former are, however, generally faint, and become associated by habit with the latter, appearing to form with it a single note of determinate pitch. These higher tones are the *harmonics* of the string, and are produced by vibrations whose numbers per second are respectively twice, three times, four times, etc., as great as those of the fundamental tone of the string. The same may be said of the notes of all instruments, including the human voice, which are usually employed for the production of musical sounds.

"16. It was stated (§ 10, p. 196) that the sound of a vibrating string was in general compounded of a number of simple tones, and a well-trained ear can detect a considerable number of them. If it were not for these harmonic components, the tones of strings, pipes, of the human voice, or, in short, of every instrument most generally used for the production of sound, would be flat and uninteresting like pure water. Each harmonic component is by itself a simple tone, and is due to the vibration of the corresponding segment of the string superposed upon that of the whole. The same statement applies *mutatis mutandis* to pipes, whether open or stopped. That the harmonics of different instruments greatly influenced their several characters is observable in the difference of the tones of a flute and clarinet. A flute is an open pipe, a clarinet a stopped one; in the former therefore the harmonics follow the order of the natural numbers 1, 2, 3, 4, and in the latter the order 1, 3, 5, 7 —the intermediate notes being supplied by opening the lateral orifices of the instrument.

"17. When two simple tones, that is (as explained above), notes deprived of all the harmonic components which under ordinary circumstances accompany them, are sounded together very nearly in unison, there are heard what are called *beats* succeeding one another at regular intervals, their rapidity depending inversely on the smallness of the interval between the two tones. Their origin may be explained thus: Suppose the tones to be produced by vibrations numbering 500 and 501 per second respectively, then every 500th sound wave of the former will strike on the tympanum at exactly the same instant as every 501st of the latter, and will reinforce it; while at the 250th of the first the corresponding wave of the other will be just half a period in front of it. Now, a sound-wave consists of a condensed and rarefied stratum of air particles, and therefore the condensed portion of one wave here coincides with the rarefied portion of the other, and neutralises it. Thus there will be an alternate reinforcement and diminution of sound, every second, from the maximum intensity when both waves impinge on the tympanum at the same instant to the minimum when they counteract each other as much as possible, and *vice versâ*.

"In the above case it was supposed that the number of vibrations of one tone were only *one* more per second than those of the other; but if the difference of the numbers had been *two*, for instance, then in one second the first tone would have gained two vibrations on the other, and there would have been two beats; and in general the number of beats per second is always equal to the difference between the two rates of vibrations per second.

"19. When the vibrations of the air due to a number of different sounds which co-exist at the same time are infinitely small, they are merely superposed one on another, so that each separate sound passes through the air as if it alone were present; and this law of superposition holds, though only approximately, until the vibrations have increased up to a certain limit, beyond which it is no longer true. Vibrations which give rise to a large amount of disturbance produce secondary waves; and it is to these that the phenomena of resultant tones are due.

"Thus if two notes a fifth apart, for instance, are forcibly sounded together, a third tone is heard an octave below the lower of the two, and this ceases to be perceptible when the loudness of the concord diminishes. In general the resultant tone of any combination of two notes is produced by a number of vibrations per second equal to the difference of the numbers per second of the notes. This fact formerly led to the supposition that the resultant tone was produced by the beats due to the consonance, which, when they occurred with sufficient rapidity, linked themselves together so as to form a continuous musical note. If this were so it is clear that the resultant ought to be heard when the original notes are sounded gently as well as forcibly; and it was the failure of this condition that led Helmholtz to the reinvestigation of their origin. These resultant tones have been named by him *difference tones;* he has also discovered the existence of resultant tones formed by the sum of the numbers of vibrations of the primaries. These *summation tones* as they are called cannot be explained on the old theory.

"20. The theory of beats explains the law that the smaller the two numbers are, which express the ratio of their vibrations, the smoother is the combination of any two tones. When two simple tones are sounded together whose rates of vibration per second differ by more than 132, the beats, according to Helmholtz, totally disappear. As the difference grows less the beats become more and more audible, the interval meanwhile growing proportionately dissonant, till they number 33 per second, at which point the dissonance of the interval is at its maximum.

"This, however, depends upon the position of the interval as regards its pitch. For it should be remembered that though the *ratio* of any given interval remains the same whatever the absolute pitch of its tones may be yet the difference of the actual numbers of their vibrations, and therefore the number of beats due to their consonance, alter with it; and *vice versâ*, if the difference of the number of vibrations remains constant, the interval must diminish as its pitch rises. For instance, either of the following combinations would give rise to 33 beats per second, since the numbers of vibrations of their tones per second, are 99-66, and 528-495, respectively. Now it is obvious that in the latter case the dissonance would be far greater than in the former.

"The above explanation of the cause of dissonance is also due to Helmholtz, and completely solves a question which had remained unanswered since the time of Pythagoras, although that philosopher made the important discovery that the simpler the ratio of the two parts into which a vibrating string was divided, the more perfect was the consonance of the two sounds.

THE END.

www.ingramcontent.com/pod-product-compliance
Lightning Source LLC
Chambersburg PA
CBHW020859230426
43666CB00008B/1236